PRAISE FOR THE WRITER'S ENCYCLOPEDIA SERIES

"I am in love with this book . . . It goes so in depth on so many tropes and gives examples of how authors use tropes to build their story. I will be using this book is to brainstorm ideas for new stories my readers will love."

-Pamela Kelley
WALL STREET JOURNAL AND USA TODAY BEST-SELLER

". . . a well-researched tool for any romance author, with each area of the book incredibly insightful and thorough. It has quickly become a staple in my business library."

-Mandi Blake
USA TODAY BEST-SELLER

"I didn't know I was looking for this exact book until I read it. Romance Character Tropes will [help authors create] characters and situations that are more complete, compelling, and satisfying for the reader."

-Ellie Hall
USA TODAY BEST-SELLER

"The authors don't just list out tropes and wish you well. Instead they provide a comprehensive and thought-provoking explanation of why conscious trope use is necessary and beneficial to your writing."

-Elizabeth Maddrey
USA TODAY BEST-SELLER

THE INSPIRED AUTHOR PRESENTS

Romance
CHARACTER TROPES

ROMANCE WRITER'S
ENCYCLOPEDIA

JESSICA BARBER
TARA G. ERICSON

This publication is designed to provide accurate and authoritative information in regard to the subject matter covered. It is sold with the understanding that neither the author nor the publisher is engaged in rendering any professional services. While the publisher and author have used their best efforts in preparing this book, they make no representations or warranties with respect to the accuracy or completeness of the contents of this book and specifically disclaim any implied warranties of merchantability or fitness for a particular purpose. No warranty may be created or extended by sales representatives or written sale materials. The advice and strategies contained herein may not be suitable for your situation. You should consult with a professional whenever appropriate. Neither the publisher nor the author should be liable for any loss of product or any other commercial, incidental, consequential, personal and other damages.

Romance Character Tropes: what readers expect from cowboys, billionaires, widows and more

Romance Writers Encyclopedia Vol 1
By Tara Grace Ericson and Jessica Barber

Print ISBN: 978-1-949896-56-5
E-book ISBN: 978-1-949896-59-6

Cover design by Tara Grace Ericson
Edited by Laurie Ingram Sibley
Printed in the United States of America
The Inspired Author Press, Rogersville,

Tara:

Dedicated to my husband—you're the only romantic hero I need.
And to the author friends who cheered me on for this project: M,H,B,J,K.
Thanks for reassuring me that this was a book that needed to be written and
that I was equipped to write it.

Jessica:

To my own cast of lowercase c *characters: the princess, the ninja, the sunshine*
girl, the rebel, and the lone wolf military hero. I love you all, and I am forever
thankful that the Lord saw fit to bless me with the most beautiful family.

ABOUT THE BOOK

In this one-of-a-kind resource, you'll find more than a list of tropes or broad advice for genre fiction.

The Romance Writer's Encyclopedia Series breaks down our method for categorizing tropes into four types of framework tropes—Character Tropes, Situational Tropes, Setting Tropes, and Relational Tropes.

This first volume of the encyclopedia includes detailed entries on favorite romance character tropes like cowboys, royalty, law enforcement, and athletes.

But this isn't just a trope list—it's an encyclopedia!

Each encyclopedia entry includes an introduction to the trope itself, as well as information on why readers love the trope, what expectations exist in the stories, common pitfalls that authors should avoid, potential wounds, and common traits.

Putting a cowboy hat on the cover of your book isn't enough to have a cowboy romance that readers will love—but we'll tell you what will. And then we'll do it for firefighters and rock stars and pirates too.

Romance Character Tropes is a book designed to be used at every stage of planning, writing, and publishing your books. If used effectively, it will help you write a romance that readers will love, but it will also help you market that book to get it into the hands of readers who will devour it.

We've studied thousands of books and movies, polled readers, and studied the market to understand not just which character tropes work—but WHY they work.

Now we're sharing that information with you, so you can use it to make your book marketable, multi-dimensional, and satisfying.

ABOUT THE AUTHORS

Best-selling author and marketing coach Tara Grace Ericson has published nearly twenty novels in Christian romance and romantic suspense. She was a Carol Award finalist for Best Christian Fiction by the American Christian Fiction Writers in 2022.

Jessica Barber is the chief editor at New Life Editing Solutions where she offers editing and story coaching services for both traditionally and independently published authors. She is the author of *Beyond the Beats: How to Write a Romance Readers Can't Resist*.

Jessica and Tara co-founded The Inspired Author in 2022 with a vision of creating books, courses, and other resources to encourage and equip authors. Learn more at www.theinspiredauthor.net

TABLE OF CONTENTS

Part One

INTRODUCTION AND GUIDE

CHAPTER 1

INTRODUCTION TO TROPES

To some writers, trope is a dirty word, marking you as a sellout genre fiction writer, pleasing the masses with predictable drivel.

To others—the informed, enlightened soul like yours? We know that tropes are not something to avoid at all costs. We know they can make the difference between a book that sells a thousand copies and a book that sells ten.

We know that even authors who profess disdain for tropifying their work will inevitably include tropes of some kind, whether they like it or not.

Let's back up though. Maybe you're neither, because this trope word people keep throwing around is just another writerly word you're afraid to ask about.

Like pantsing.

Or NaNo.

CHAPTER 1

Or why everyone has so many WIPs? Do you need a safe word? (Admittedly, that joke is funnier in audio, but you got it, right?)

Let's untangle this literary term which gets thrown around so often.

WHAT IS A TROPE?

To put it in the most basic terms, a literary trope is any element that is used many times by many different writers. These elements include figures of speech, themes, symbols, settings, characters, or plot devices. Tropes have been used throughout the entire history of the written world, across cultures, genres, and yes, even in literary fiction.

In a broad sense, tropes are the very product of the saying, "There is nothing new under the sun." As writers, we know that can be a bit discouraging. How can my story be unique and interesting if everything has already been done?

The truth actually lies somewhere in the middle of the two. Your story will never be exactly like any other story. Because no other writer is exactly like you. But your story is guaranteed to share elements with hundreds of storytellers reaching back generations.

Your novel may take place in a fictional land, unlike any other ever written, where people travel on giant bunnies and fight battles by blowing poison bubbles at one another. But tropes like The Chosen One or Unlikely Band of Heroes are likely to sneak into your manuscript, even if you have no idea what they are.

It's okay!

This is NOT a bad thing.

As a storyteller, you may profess to love them or hate them, but the truth is tropes exist for a reason. They've been repeated in stories again and again because they are compelling to the audience. From the beginning of civilization, there has always been something exciting about hearing a story of a normal (often orphaned) boy finding out he has extraordinary gifts and an adventure waiting for him (see *Harry Potter*, *Percy Jackson and the Olympians*, *Star Wars*, King David in the Bible). A forbidden love affair makes us hold our breath, waiting for the other shoe to drop—whether it is feuding families or a regal prince disobeying his father and falling for the servant girl (see *West Side Story*, *Titanic*, or *Twilight*).

OUR GOAL IS TO HELP YOU UNDERSTAND THE PURPOSE OF THE TROPES, IDENTIFY THE KEY ELEMENTS OF POPULAR TROPES, AND TEACH YOU HOW TO UTILIZE THEM EFFECTIVELY

Tropes exist in all genres of fiction, but in this series, we will specifically dive into tropes within the romance genre.

Can you think back to the first romantic movie you remember loving? If you were a 90s kid, maybe it was *She's All That* with a young Freddie Prinze Jr. Or, if you're older, perhaps it was *Pretty Woman* or *Dirty Dancing*, *The Way We Were* or *My Fair Lady*. If we leave the big screen, we could look at books: from Shakespeare to Jane Austen to Nora Roberts. All of these works use tropes as tools for engaging their audience, shaping characters and conflict, and deepening the story.

Earlier, we defined a trope as a repeated element of speech, themes, symbols, settings, characters, or plot. We will focus on character tropes in this book, with the other elements being mentioned only when relevant to the character trope. Our goal is to help you understand the purpose of the tropes, identify the key elements of popular tropes, and teach you how to utilize them effectively in your writing to create a story that captures your readers' attention and delivers on the unwritten expectations each trope promises without being predictable, cookie cutter, or derivative.

A Note from the Authors

Before we start, there's something you should know. Here at The Inspired Author, we LOVE romance, but we don't do steam. It's not something we write, read, or enjoy based on our personal faith convictions. This isn't a book to bash or exclude authors and readers of steamy romance, but you won't find it addressed in any of the Inspired Author Network materials.

As we take apart the tropes one-by-one, you might think we've missed something crucial. In many cases, it will probably be true because we're human, but especially when it comes to things that are unique to the expectations of steamy romance. While we still think much of this book will be relevant to the higher-steam market, just know that there MAY be steam-related expectations of the trope that we don't cover.

We are speaking from our places of expertise in sweet, clean, or inspirational romance, so don't expect to find Trope Encyclopedia entries based on tropes that are unique to steamy or dark romance (such as Why Choose/Reverse Harem,

Mafia, or Bully romance). You can, however, extrapolate the material in our encyclopedias to create your own set of reader expectations, fulfilled reader desires, and pitfalls that are relevant for these other tropes. Hopefully, the content of this book will make you feel well-equipped for such a task.

Learning how the framework of these trope categories works will help you to dissect any trope you may encounter in your reading or writing. And reading a few of your favorite books using this trope will allow you to identify what makes it work, the most exciting and memorable elements for you as a reader, and how the trope is driving the story.

All that said, let's examine some myths about tropes before we go deeper into character tropes specifically.

CHAPTER 2

THE PURPOSE OF TROPES
(What Tropes Do and Do Not)

---

*Tropes DO NOT build the
foundation of your story.*

Jane Austen didn't sit down with a list of plot devices, scan the list, and think, "I'll write an **Enemies to Lovers** story today." What she did was create deep, rich characters with a complex transformation arc who happen to also move from outright disdain (in the delightfully complex subtext of proper society) to "ardent admiration."

The main trope in *Pride and Prejudice* of **Enemies to Lovers** serves the story of a proud, arrogant man and a witty, stubborn woman. Characters and emotional arcs should be the foundation of a story. The relational trope of **Enemies to Lovers** is a way to help provide the context and conflict for that transformation to take place. The setting trope of regency England also provides unique challenges and situations for the characters' journey to unfold.

Tropes have developed over time because they are elements that audiences have connected with. But without well-rounded characters, emotional connection, and conflict, even stories that hit every trope just fall flat. In each book, we'll address how the type of trope works as a framework *on which to build* the foundation of your story.

The primary unit of story is the plot, or the sequence of events. The plot will be influenced by elements such as genre, premise, and— you guessed it—tropes. The plot includes the central conflict, the actions and decisions of the characters, and the resolution of the conflict. But plot alone will not give your story the solid foundation that it needs; it needs the support of characters, setting, and theme. Together these elements create the foundation of a story, providing a structure that supports the narrative and guides the reader through the events that unfold.

By creating a sense of familiarity and shaping reader expectations, tropes provide a valuable framework for the plot. They can influence plot structure or provide archetypes and themes which can be used to craft a compelling narrative. Layering tropes can maximize their effect on your story's foundation. A situational trope can flesh out the conflict, and a character trope can develop a strong character arc and backstory.

Tropes DO make promises to the reader.

Whether readers acknowledge it or not, they carry expectations into every book they read. It might be based on a familiar author. It might be based on the cover or the title or the blurb. For some genres, the expectation might even be that the reader "expects" to be totally surprised. But for romance, we all know there is one GIANT expectation: This couple will end up together in a happily ever after (HEA) or a happy for now (HFN) by the end of the story.

Romance readers have other expectations, often laid by the trope. If you pick up a story where a woman is falling for her brother's best friend, you have the general expectation that there will be some conflict about how the brother will react or some reason the couple will want to keep things low-key. If that unwritten expectation isn't met, the reader may finish a totally enjoyable romance and feel like there was something missing. They might not even be able to articulate why they felt let down by the story—but it's because the setup promised something that the story didn't deliver.

This is why authors can write books that deliver the same things over and over again and have readers eagerly awaiting their next book. The author promised a cowboy romance, and that is exactly what the reader happily received.

By intentionally choosing the tropes and delivering what was promised, you build trust with the reader. And while we might think readers don't want to know what they are getting in a story, the market dynamics tell us the exact opposite. Readers want "familiar but different" stories—which brings us to the next function of tropes.

11

Tropes DO provide
"familiar but different" stories.

We've already established that it's the familiarity of tropes that resonates so strongly with readers—but it is the variation, the twists and the subversions that create a fresh and unique take on a well-loved story and a compelling narrative. We like to think of any good story as a tapestry. Every author's story will look different. They'll choose different colors and different patterns to tie it all together. They might even choose different fibers. Even if they start with the same end goal—to make a tapestry—how they get there will be completely different.

But tropes help add something familiar to the tapestry of a story that the reader is examining. It might be the setting of an idyllic small town that they are drawn to, or the setup of a workplace romance with the undercurrents of an off-limits relationship that they can't resist.

The rest of the story will still be unique, infused with the artistic touch of the author, but a reader will naturally be drawn to something within the story that is slightly familiar.

Tropes help us create a framework for our tapestry. Something creative and different, but not so different that a reader is confused and hesitant to buy it. It allows the reader to look at the story and latch onto something they enjoy so they are willing to take a risk on the rest. That's what we want as authors. They have to be intrigued with the premise enough to have a chance to fall in love with the story, and in turn—the author.

---

*Tropes CAN fulfill common
reader wishes or desires.*

One of the biggest things we will do in Part 3 of this book is examine different tropes and dive into why readers love stories featuring that trope. What we'll find is that so many tropes can be traced back to some deep longing or wish within the reader. And many of these are generally shared by the larger population.

Why set your story in a **Small Town**? A longing for simpler times and a place where people truly know and appreciate each other.

Why **Law Enforcement**, **Bodyguards**, **Firefighters**, and **Military**? A deeper wish for protection and provision from a strong, honorable hero.

Why **Friends to More**? An underlying desire to have a romantic relationship with the person who understands you better than anyone in the whole world.

Why **Fake Relationship**? The longing for a life with a little more drama—for shared secrets and being "on the inside" of the excitement.

There are more of course, and perhaps not all tropes tie into a secret wish of the reader, but we would argue that most do. And by acknowledging that and leveraging that secret longing—you can make your book satisfy ALL those deeper, unacknowledged desires. And you can use them in your marketing to make your book irresistible.

Tropes DO NOT make up for lazy writing.

Please don't misunderstand us. We do not want you to slap a few tropes together, add a kiss here and there, and call it a romance. Even the most powerful tropes will not save your manuscript from lazy writing, cookie-cutter characters, lackluster conflict, poor grammar or editing, or any other number of writing and publishing pitfalls!

Well executed tropes will elevate your story, make it easier to sell, and give readers a more satisfying ending.

But you still have to write the story.

You still have to make it engaging.

WELL EXECUTED TROPES WILL ELEVATE YOUR STORY, MAKE IT EASIER TO SELL, AND GIVE READERS A MORE SATISFYING ENDING

You still have to make the reader feel the pain, the angst, the joy, and the excitement of falling in love and reaching the end goal.

A trope cannot do that for you. It can help set up the framework for a good story. But in and of itself, a trope will not carry you.

If you want to work on other aspects of your craft, we recommend reading *Beyond the Beats* by Jessica Barber. It covers everything from conflict to backstory and specific elements of prose such as effective dialogue and description.

*Tropes DO NOT mean an author
has to "plot" their story.*

One of the most unique aspects of our relationship (that is, the relationship of your authors, Jessica and Tara) is our completely different approach to writing stories. Jessica is a proud plotter. Tara, despite multiple attempts to put on a plotter mentality, has embraced her intuitive nature to proclaim herself a pantser.

One of the things we have come to understand about plotting or pantsing or anywhere in between, is that a deeper understanding of story and conflict and characters is beneficial no matter which point in the process those pieces of information are put into play. The same goes with tropes. Perhaps, like Jessica, you want to know exactly where the story is going before you ever start writing. Which means, you identify the tropes ahead of time and can be very intentional about adding the conflict, emotion, romance, and world building into the story.

For the rest of us though, we can still use tropes super effectively!

For some, it might be more intuitive, and you might not recognize you were utilizing a specific trope until it shows up in the manuscript. Or perhaps you are a premise writer—so you know ahead of time the two people you are matching and the scenario or relationship that will bring them together. In either case, you might want to flesh out the trope and expectations during the editing phase so it is as powerful as it can be.

CHAPTER 3

THE CATEGORIES OF
FRAMEWORK TROPES

We are far from the first people to compile and categorize tropes, especially romance tropes. We've seen and used many of those lists—and they absolutely *can* be helpful. Heck, we even created our own (and this is our shameless plug for The Inspired Author *Ultimate Romance Trope List*). But as we talked extensively about what we saw happening in the romance market, we realized the problem wasn't that people couldn't recognize specific tropes, or even why they are a functional element of story.

The issue we saw time and again when editing, story coaching, and offering marketing and business consultations was that authors didn't understand *how* tropes were functioning in their story. What made one **Billionaire** romance a success and the other a total flop? Even among talented writers, or authors using similar covers and the same blurb writer!

What we discovered was how different tropes interacted and impacted the story. And quickly, the four categories of romance tropes became very clear to us. These four categories are the basis for the first four volumes of this series, and we think it's important for you to understand *why* we've chosen to break them down like this.

The four categories are as follows:

CHARACTER TROPES

On the surface, these tropes may seem like nothing more than a label, but when done well, your choice of character trope will significantly impact the development of your character arcs. They will inform your choice of attributes, and they will affect the way your character responds to their situation and the actions of others.

These are extremely powerful marketing tools, and authors can build entire careers on one single character trope. There is a reason we chose to make character tropes the first volume of the Romance Writer's Encyclopedia. They are *that* important. In this volume, we'll discuss over thirty character tropes—what they are, what makes them work and why they fail.

SETTING TROPES

Setting tropes play a major role in the world building of your book or series. They can aid you in description of place, time, customs, and archetypes. Place and time may indicate the region, the type of environment (like urban or small town), and time period. Most setting tropes also carry specific side character archetypes like the small-town busybody, the regency wallflower, or the western sheriff.

In addition to this, elements like figures of speech, colloquialisms, local dress, and customs will all be heavily influenced by the setting trope you choose. We'd all be surprised to see your beach bunny heroine show up to the meet-cute in a parka—and if your hero is a mountain man, your readers will have to give up their dreams of finding him wandering the woods in a tuxedo. Many readers choose books exclusively based on the setting tropes, and creating the setting as a character itself is a powerful tool to draw readers in and keep them coming back book after book.

RELATIONAL TROPES

When tropes are discussed, relational tropes often top the lists— we're talking **Friends to More**, **Enemies to Lovers**, **Second Chance**, or **Childhood Sweethearts**. These tropes are all about how the character's existing relationship will influence the romance arc as the narrative develops. They will play a role in major story beats such as the meet cute, midpoint, and black moment (also known as dark night of the soul).

The key to these tropes lies in the shifting of values on what we call a "hate-to-love scale." This means that as your characters progress through scenes, chapters, and acts, there should be a change in attitude toward one another. These values will start somewhere on the negative side of the spectrum, which spans hate to disinterest, eventually making their way through the stages of attraction, intimacy, and commitment. Each trope in this category will move through the scale differently, but each will end at their happily ever after.

CHAPTER 3

STORYLINE TROPES

Storyline tropes will drive the external plot and conflict of your story, and like relational tropes, these are some of the most commonly discussed. They may also influence critical story beats, and they will inform the progression and content of your scenes. Most of these will be adhesion tropes that force our characters together and make it oh-so-fun to read. Some examples include **Marriage of Convenience**, **Fake Relationship**, **Forced Proximity**, and **Renovation**.

* * *

That's it! Remember, there are tons of tropes that don't fall into these categories, since tropes are any element used many times by many authors. A kiss in the rain is a trope. But in the grand scheme of your book, it is far less likely to impact a full arc or major part of your story. Same for the swoony, protective *Who did this to you?* line when the heroine is hurt. These are delicious little fun scenes within a story, but they aren't *framework* tropes, and that's what we want to focus on here.

If you're looking for a list of these framework tropes broken down into these categories, but you don't want to wait for or reference four separate books, our easy-to-download "Ultimate Romance Trope List" is available as a PDF on The Inspired Author website. It also includes a quick reference guide for combining and layering tropes—but let's go into a little more depth here.

MIXING AND LAYERING TROPES

When looking to add depth, complexity, and tension to your romance story, one of the most effective methods is to layer tropes, allowing you to craft a narrative that engages readers on multiple levels. If the idea is to avoid your reader picking up the blurb and thinking "I've read this book before," then we need to break the formula and create something unique. Layering tropes allows us to do this.

Looking at things from a numbers perspective, you might say there are X number of romance books that feature **Marriage of Convenience**, Y number of stories with a **Small Town** setting, and Z with **Brother's Best Friend** . . . but how many books will feature all three of those tropes working in tandem? That number is going to be much smaller, making your story a truly unique experience for the reader. Not to mention, authors who find their niche in a single trope, or series that utilize the same trope for several books—if each book feels like a carbon copy with nothing more than different names and slightly different sources of conflict, readers are likely to stay engaged through an entire series.

ONE OF THE MOST EFFECTIVE METHODS TO ADD DEPTH, COMPLEXITY, AND TENSION TO YOUR STORY IS TO LAYER TROPES

To start mixing tropes, think about which ones lend themselves easily to others in different categories. You'll find a helpful chart of "commonly paired with" tropes in each encyclopedia entry. These ideas may be used to guide your selection of tropes, or you can shake things up and surprise your reader with two tropes they don't expect to see together (such as an **Urban Cowboy**).

21

Consider options like combining two character tropes into an enigmatic **Lone Wolf Billionaire** or leaning into two separate character tropes in the unexpected romance between a **Rich Girl** and a **Bad Boy**. You could do the same with any framework trope, whether relational, situational or even setting-related.

You might ask yourself a few *what if* questions to drum up some intriguing possibilities. What if your characters had a shared history? What if they were forced to collaborate despite their differences? What if they found themselves stranded in a challenging situation together? These questions lay the groundwork for weaving intricate layers of tension and connection.

For an even more captivating tale, don't limit yourself to a single framework category—mix and match tropes from different categories to construct a rich tapestry of elements. This systematic approach not only stimulates your authorial creativity but also generates unique and appealing story premises.

A NOTE FROM YOUR MARKETING COACH

When mixing tropes within the same category, keep in mind that some tropes stack better than others. Often those that form their own browsing categories (like **Cowboy** or **Billionaire**) are more likely to stack well with another trope from the same framework category. Incorporating multiple tropes from a single framework category can further enhance the complexity of your narrative.

-TGE

Here are a few examples to illustrate the process:

Character + Relational + Situational + Setting

Cowboy + Best Friend's Sister + Marriage of Convenience + Christmas:

A rugged cowboy finds himself in an unexpected situation—entering into a marriage of convenience with his best friend's sister, all against the backdrop of the heartwarming Christmas season. This combination offers a blend of familial tension, personal growth, and festive charm.

Hero Character (x2) + Heroine Character + Situational/Setting

Single Dad Billionaire + Nanny/Caregiver + Road Trip:

Explore the journey of a single dad billionaire and his children as they embark on a transformative road trip with a nanny who becomes much more than just a caregiver. This trope mix promises a blend of emotional growth, unexpected connections, and a dynamic change of scenery.

Hero Character + Relational + Situational + Setting

NFL Player + Best Friends + Jilted Bride + Beach Town:

Dive into a narrative where an NFL player seeks refuge in a tranquil beach town, finding solace in his best friend's company—who was recently left at the altar by her fiancé. Against the backdrop of the beach town, their friendship evolves into a deeper connection, igniting a tale of healing, loyalty, and newfound romance.

CHAPTER 3

***

Identifying a trope for your story doesn't have to be hard! Choosing one or two from each category can help you make sure your story has a balance of character growth, conflict, tension, adhesion, and worldbuilding. Not every story needs a trope from each category, especially if the others are prominent or pack a strong punch on their own. (Check out Case Study 3 for an example of a successful movie with almost nothing but character tropes!) However, you might find that bringing in a separate category of framework trope fills in the gaps of your narrative that you've been struggling with.

By crafting a story premise using a main character trope that resonates with readers, a relational trope that fuels romantic tension, a situational trope that draws characters together, and a captivating setting where everything will unfold, you set the stage for a compelling narrative.

While not every trope combination will be successful, and some might have been explored before, remember that you, as the author, have the power to infuse your unique perspective and creative voice into the story, making it your own.

CHAPTER 4

HOW TO USE THIS BOOK

Romance Character Tropes will aim to provide more than just a list of tropes. Our goal is to give you an in-depth breakdown of some of the most widely used character tropes.

With each entry, we will introduce and define the trope, so we are all speaking the same language. Then we'll dissect what it is that readers love about the trope, spoken and unspoken expectations of the trope, and common pitfalls. We'll talk about related tropes or framework tropes it is commonly paired with (so you can decide to play into that or twist it). In Part 4, we'll pick a few popular movies and break down the successful use of character tropes in that film.

These books are intended to be used at every stage of planning, writing, and publishing your books. If used effectively, the Romance Writer's Encyclopedia series will help you write a romance that readers will love, and it will also help you market that book to get it into the hands of readers who will devour it.

In Part 3, we've broken down more than thirty of the most popular character tropes of romances. Some you might know, and others are less common but still beloved by readers. We've grouped similar characters together; for example, much of the information about royalty also applies to billionaires, but we've also included sections about how each specific trope is unique.

TO BRAINSTORM AND PLAN YOUR BOOKS

The Character Trope Encyclopedia will help spark ideas for you while plotting or planning the premise. Each section will give you ideas for how to fulfill reader expectations, breathe fresh life into a story, and maybe even combine tropes in new ways. The information in this book may help you decide what to write through our shared research into which tropes are the most popular, which are underserved, which tropes may be best utilized to help you set up a successful book or series with intentional choices.

TO EDIT YOUR BOOKS

While drafting or editing your book, the encyclopedia entries serve as an excellent source to double check whether you are hitting the mark for the intended trope. With common traits, potential wounds, and pitfalls in easy-to-reference entries, you can use the encyclopedia to home in on the reader expectations for the trope and make small adjustments to your manuscript that will have a big impact on the reader experience. These changes don't always require an entire rewrite—you may be surprised what a few well-placed new lines of prose or dialogue can do to round out elements such as character or conflict!

TO MARKET YOUR BOOKS

Character tropes are one of the most powerful marketing tools available to authors today. Using the information in the encyclopedia about WHY readers love each trope will help you craft your marketing content, write an effective sales blurb, and hook readers before they even crack the cover. Elements such as title and subtitle, cover design, and keywords or browsing categories can get a major boost by capitalizing on the prominent tropes in your work.

But this isn't a trope list. This is an encyclopedia. So let's dive into character tropes.

Part Two

CHARACTER TROPES
IN ROMANCE

CHAPTER 5

INTRODUCTION TO
CHARACTER TROPES

If you remember our definition of a trope (any story element—including figures of speech, theme, setting, character, or plot devices—that is used many times by many different writers), the definition of a character trope becomes pretty evident.

A character trope is a *type of character* used many times by many different writers. Character tropes may include recurring and recognizable patterns which can be found in all mediums of storytelling (novels, movies, tv shows.) It's a shorthand way to quickly convey certain traits, behaviors, or roles associated with a specific type of character.

Now, that obviously doesn't mean the author isn't creating unique, varied versions of a character trope. You'll see us using a capital *C* Character when we are referring to the trope, and a lowercase *c* character, when referring to the unique version of this person in your book.

But calling your character a **Billionaire** isn't enough to make the trope effective in marketing or storytelling, and character tropes encompass so much more than just interesting personalities and careers. It goes deeper than that, which is why we've created this encyclopedia. First of all, we need to talk about how to turn your **Billionaire** (or **Cowboy** or **Widow**) into a living, breathing character that readers want to explore.

By informing your choice of attributes, social behaviors and even backstory and potential wounds, the tools for building your c character will be directly influenced by the hallmarks of the C Character you choose to model. Readers will be drawn to your characters,

> CHARACTER TROPES WILL AFFECT THE WAY YOUR PROTAGONIST APPROACHES AND REACTS TO THEIR CIRCUMSTANCES, HOW THEY INTERACT WITH OTHERS AND ULTIMATELY WHAT IT TAKES FOR THEM TO OVERCOME THE OBSTACLES TO A LASTING LOVE

because they already know they love so many of the storytelling elements you've incorporated, and you've let them know what they can expect through marketing elements like the title, cover, and back copy (or Amazon description).

While these tropes do help audiences identify and understand characters more easily, they can also lead to clichés or predictable storytelling if overused. The romance genre shares plenty of character tropes with other genres, but there are a few we will discuss that are unique or presented in a somewhat different light when it comes to love stories. Regardless of how many stories a character trope may show up in, we'll discuss how they are shaped by the reader expectations of a romance novel and how they influence other story elements such as conflict and relationship arc.

The character tropes you will encounter in this book should influence the character development of your hero or heroine. They will affect the way your protagonist approaches and reacts to their circumstances, how they interact with others, and ultimately what it takes for them to overcome the obstacles to a lasting love. These character tropes provide a familiar framework that readers can engage with, allowing you as the writer to create relatable character journeys.

Here are some of the ways tropes can affect the character arc in your romance story:

Starting Point and Expectations: Readers come to the story with a preconceived understanding of the characters' roles based on your chosen trope. This provides a starting point for the characters' initial circumstances, personalities, their relationships, and interactions.

Conflict and Growth: Character arcs in romance stories must involve personal transformation, and the trope you choose will influence how that transformation unfolds. As conflicts and challenges are introduced, the way your character responds will be directly linked to the dynamics and characteristics of your chosen trope. As characters navigate these challenges, they experience growth and development.

Resolution and Satisfaction: Tropes guide the resolution of conflicts and the ultimate outcome of the romance. Readers expect a certain type of resolution based on the values, motivations, and reactions inherent to the character trope.

Subversion and Innovation: As you begin to master these tropes in their most conventional forms, you will also learn to use tropes that subvert expectations and add depth to character arcs. By putting a unique twist on familiar tropes, you can challenge stereotypes and deliver unexpected character growth. In doing so, you can leverage any given trope in order to create engaging and relatable journeys for your characters while adding your own creative twist. Trope subversions and pitfalls are further discussed in Chapter 9.

CHARACTER TROPES AND THE FOUNDATION OF YOUR STORY

This entire series of Trope Encyclopedias will serve to show you, writer, that tropes are an excellent tool to utilize when laying the framework of your narrative, but they are not solid enough to carry it. Hear us when we say *Tropes should serve your story, not the other way around.* As the author, your job is to take a character trope and create an interesting, unique, and well-rounded character. Whether you plot, premise, or

> TROPES SHOULD SERVE YOUR STORY, NOT THE OTHER WAY AROUND—AS THE AUTHOR YOUR JOB IS TO TAKE A CHARACTER TROPE AND CREATE A UNIQUE, INTERESTING, AND WELL-ROUNDED CHARACTER

pants—your (lowercase) character is more than a cardboard cutout with the label of whatever character trope you land on.

While character tropes will feed into characters and have a direct influence on the transformation of your main character, and as a result, the rest of the story, you will need to build up the other key

A NOTE FROM YOUR STORY COACH

elements of story—plot, conflict, theme and the relational arc. This book won't necessarily discuss each of these elements in depth, but for further study, we highly recommend Jessica Barber's *Beyond the Beats* and *Dramatica* by Chris Huntley and Melanie Anne Phillips.

Narrative elements such as author voice, writing style, and point of view will combine with the foundation of your story to make each book distinct, despite an abundance of shared tropes. Many of these elements will be influenced by choices such as subgenre and trope, but ultimately you, as the author, get to choose to either subvert expectations or embrace them, adding your unique spin to create a fresh and engaging story.

Establish clear motivations for each character beyond the trope itself. What do they want? What fears or obstacles do they face? This helps humanize them and drive the story.

Allow both characters to grow individually and together throughout the story. Their development should extend beyond the trope, reflecting their unique experiences and challenges.

-JB

Relying solely on tropes can not only lead to predictability, but it can also result in poorly fleshed out conflict, shallow characters, and a disconnect between theme and plot. Providing nuanced perspectives on relationships and exploring themes beyond romance alone will take the framework of your trope and allow you to build a compelling and memorable narrative. As you flesh out your character with distinct personalities, motivations, and flaws, their emotional journey will easily align with reader expectations. And the dynamic formed by bringing together two unique and interesting characters results in a romance arc that deeply resonates with your readers. As these characters navigate challenges, discover their feelings, and find love and fulfillment, the heart of your narrative will shine through, and the resulting tension and intimacy will be shaped by the way you bring together all the elements of your framework tropes.

While much of your character's personality and worldview will be tied to the trope you choose, there is plenty of room for variation to come in through past experience, trauma, and wounds. You can add further depth to your character's internal conflict, both personal and romantic, through their desires, motivations, and insecurities, and by subverting trope expectations (more on that later).

The way that your characters interact, speak to one another and share experiences will be influenced by the tropes you choose, but gradually it should lead to the development of intimacy, desire, and an unbreakable bond. This bond needs to be believable and engaging, so it is worth considering the compatibility or dissonance between character types. As the complexities of your hero and heroine's personalities collide or strengthen one another, it will lead to transformation of the relationship and ultimately transformation of your characters. The reader should authentically connect with the emotions of your characters so that they feel the highs and lows along with the characters. This means you will want to maintain a balance between these moments of connection and moments of tension in order for the development of the relationship to feel genuine and build the reader's investment in the outcome.

Theme will ultimately be the connection between your character's progression and conflict (internal, external, and relational). By considering a central message that stems naturally from the character tropes in your story, you amplify the ability for your readers to relate or empathize with it.

How character tropes might influence these key elements:

- some tropes like **Cowboy, Pirate,** or **Musician** will lend themselves to world building, setting, atmosphere, and mood
- character-specific traits will influence interactions, relationships, actions, and reactions to circumstances
- internal conflict is prominent in specific tropes (such as **Bad Boy, Lone Wolf,** or **Rags to Riches**)
- relationship dynamics may be influenced by shared experiences with love interests or supporting characters who fall under similar tropes or come from similar background
- mixing character tropes can lead to tension, conflict, and shifting relationship dynamics (**Lumberjack** paired with **Rags to Riches** heroine for example).

Your character's personality will come from many places, and in fact, some personality archetypes have turned into character tropes in and of themselves. We'll call those Internal Character Tropes (examples would be **Alpha Male, Bad Boy,** or **Damsel in Distress**). These character tropes are mostly related to character personality and interaction styles. If you're looking for more resources on types of heroes as far as personality and characteristics, check out *The Complete Writer's Guide to Heroes and Heroines: Sixteen Master Archetypes* by Tami D. Cowden, Caro LaFever, and Sue Viders.

For most of Part 3, we will focus on External Character Tropes, because those are generally bigger framework tropes. These will be the tropes determined by your character's career or life stage, and you may find these options somewhat more flexible for crafting a one-of-a-kind story.

CHAPTER 5

External Character Tropes (such as **Cowboy**, **Billionaire**, **Athlete**, **Widow**, or **Doctor**) will incorporate factors beyond the character's career or stage of life to encompass priorities, personality, and even their story world. They are not necessarily derived from archetypes. (Although some of them do pair nicely or closely relate to specific archetypes!) Both Internal and External Character Tropes can be used as marketing tools as well as inform the character arc and conflict of your story.

Personality, backstory, goals, and motivation turn your Character into a character that readers want to read. We see these Characters all the time in movies, television shows, and books. We recognize them, and there is something within us (the reader or watcher) that makes us want to hear their story. More about that in the section on "Reader Wish Fulfillment." For more resources on how to do that, we recommend K.M. Weiland's *Creating Character Arcs*, Jessica Barber's *Beyond the Beats*, and Marshall Dotson's *Actions and Goals*.

CHAPTER 6

CREATING COMPLEX CHARACTERS

Your characters have idiosyncrasies and preferences like any person you come across in your real life. What makes them unique? What do their friends tease them about?

Ensure that all your characters, especially the love interests, possess strong inner motivations. A well-defined sense of purpose and desire will make them more engaging and relatable to readers, drawing them deeper into the story. Avoid weak or one-dimensional love interests, as they may dampen the overall appeal of the romance. Most of all, they have goals and a motivation for those goals. Not only that, but their stated motivation is often the result of some hidden, unspoken motive or fear.

For example, the capital *B* Billionaire who wants to achieve ultimate success is boring. Until you find out that the reason he strives so hard is because he is still seeking his father's approval (whether he admits it to himself or not). That makes your boring Billionaire into a relatable billionaire that readers empathize with.

Same for a cowboy. Until you, the author (and subsequently, the reader), understand what makes your capital *C* Cowboy want to save the family ranch from bankruptcy or win a gold belt by getting on the back of a crazy bull, he's just flat. And readers will find that there is nothing especially memorable about your Cowboy romance.

In order to create complex characters with emotional depth, strengths, and weaknesses, the growth arc should be the central focus anytime you consider how their trope will shape and impact the story.

WHILE VULNERABILITIES, FEARS, AND PAST HURT WILL BE UNIQUE TO YOUR CHARACTER, THERE ARE CERTAIN VALUES AND MOTIVATIONS THAT WILL BE HUGELY INFLUENCED BY THEIR TROPE

As the narrative progresses, allow them to evolve beyond their initial trope-driven traits. This transformation should resonate organically with their experiences and challenges. By layering and combining multiple character tropes (such as internal and external), you can create more nuance and dimension to your character through a multifaceted personality and rich backstory. While the values of these tropes may clash in such a way that they intensify your hero or heroine's internal struggle, keep in mind that they should also be coherent in the way they influence and complement one another—most of us are not writing schizophrenics. No matter how you choose to layer character tropes (or even if you choose not to), ensure that your characters are consistent and that their choices make sense.

Your character's arc will be shaped by their actions and reactions to the events of the story, but the way that they respond to these forces (both internal and external) should ring true to the character trope you've chosen. While the vulnerabilities, fears, and past hurt will be unique to your character, there are certain values and motivations that will be hugely influenced by their trope. A rancher, for example, is unlikely to take an action that will result in the loss of his property and herd without some serious internal struggle. A billionaire will be motivated by the desire to maintain his lifestyle, success, or reputation. And even if a recluse needs to meet his heroine at some point, he is unlikely to push himself out of his comfort zone and attend a large gathering without some serious external force and subsequent soul searching—even then, we're sure he's not happy about it.

Your tropes will lend themselves well to creating strengths and weaknesses for your character so that you can create complex, flawed, and compelling characters. Other commonly used tools when building (or discovering) your character's personality are personality tests like Meyers-Briggs, DISC, or CliftonStrengths. Childhood experiences and trauma can impact personality as well.

There are three things you should seek to achieve in order to develop unique and memorable characters:

1) For the reader to be seen and heard (this is where wish fulfillment comes in)
2) For the reader to be immersed (internal dialogue and direct discourse go a long way on this front)
3) For the reader to believe the character might be real (read the trope entries closely, and this one will be a shoo-in)

Take your character beyond the initial trope-driven traits. As the story unfolds, they should grow, learn, and change in response the events and challenges they overcome, and this should feel organic and authentic to your character's journey. Use dialogue and internal dialogue to provide insights into thoughts and emotions and offer glimpses into their internal complexity. Remember that the way your character speaks will be a factor of the era, education, personality, and culture, so diction, pacing, word choice, and idioms should be considered accordingly. The ultimate aim is to strike a balance by enriching the character tropes with layers of authenticity.

In the rest of this chapter, you will find points to consider and methods for creating characters that capture the interest of readers.

Embrace classic archetypes as a starting point. Each archetype carries its set of recognizable traits and behaviors that readers can readily identify. Archetypes will be adapted through the lens of the romance genre in Chapter 11 as Internal Character Tropes, but studying archetypes can help you to delve deeper into what makes your character *universally* relatable and engaging to the reader.

Highlight motivations and goals that go beyond the obvious character trope traits (though they should still make sense given the trope you choose). Consider desires, fears, and aspirations. What drives them, and what do they truly want? Is it what they really need?

Create complexity by adding in layers to foundational traits. Consider how your character's motivations, fears, and vulnerabilities as well as their backstory/past experiences, traumas, and personal history will shape their behavior and interactions. Complexity can also stem from conflicting desires; often these result from layering more than one trope or subverting the trope.

Use flashback scenes or allude to them through internal dialogue or direct discourse to reveal pivotal moments from a character's past that shaped them into the character they've become. This gives the reader insight into their development and deepens their ability to empathize.

Challenge your character with internal conflicts that disrupt the alignment with the trope. For instance, a **Reformed Bad Boy** might wrestle with lingering impulses from his past, a struggle which will be intensified by his growing desire for genuine connection with the love interest.

COMPLEXITY CAN ALSO STEM FROM CONFLICTING DESIRES WHICH OFTEN RESULT FROM SUBVERTING A TROPE OR LAYERING MORE THAN ONE TROPE

A little bit of moral ambiguity can allow your character to make difficult choices that challenge their traditional role or personality type. It can forge unexpected bonds or relationships and push them out of their comfort zone, but ultimately these changes should lead to a shift that pushes them further along in their character arc. What will your character learn from the situation? How will it reinforce or reject the worldview that stems from the character trope?

Subvert reader expectations by introducing unexpected traits or behaviors that pique the readers' interest and defy typical stereotype-associated behaviors (raise your hand if you'd swoon for a bad boy who knows how to crochet). This is one of the most effective ways to break away from one-dimensional or cliché character types.

Explore how relationship dynamics associated with your trope influence character growth and emotional evolution. How does their character trope affect the connections they form? Consider the character trope of the love interest—how do their personal journeys intersect and affect each other? Are their tendencies and personalities at odds, or do they complement each other well?

Highlight the vulnerabilities and wounds which may result from the trope. They humanize them, foster reader connections, and establish emotional investment in the character and romance.

To delve into how their occupational environment influences their journey, consider key questions about their career trajectory, job satisfaction, and any past traumatic experiences related to their profession. Additionally, explore how their career either fulfills their perceived needs or reveals their true needs, acting as either an obstacle or a catalyst in their development.

It is essential to remember that tropes should not be superficial marketing gimmicks; instead, they should profoundly influence the character's choices and actions. If a protagonist holds a specific occupation, it must significantly impact their characterization and decision-making, reflecting a realistic and authentic application of the trope.

CHAPTER 7

CHARACTER TROPES
AND CONFLICT

Conflict is the key agent of change in stories of all genres, and it goes hand in hand with both plot structure and character (tropes).

The character tropes you employ should play a significant role in shaping the conflict of your romance story by providing the foundation for character dynamics, interactions, and obstacles. It is the conflicts that arise over the course of your narrative plot that challenges your characters and forces them out of their comfort zone to confront their flaws and weaknesses.

Character development isn't a linear process, and setbacks and challenges can be just as important as successes. So, using conflict to push your characters to grow and change even further, you can demonstrate their resilience and determination. When we also take into account their character trope, past experiences, current circumstances, and the various aspects of personality and belief system, it creates an atmosphere rife for conflict and tension. With regard to tropes, the values and priorities of your character will either be affirmed or rejected based on the outcome of facing these challenges.

At the core of any conflict arc in a romance novel, you will have two people whose worlds have collided in such a way that they are now forced to reconcile their own internal and external goals with an irresistible pull to the union with their love interest. As we've discussed in other sections, the elements of each character's internal or external character trope may complement each other, making them a force to be reckoned with, or they may collide, requiring some sort of sacrifice by one or both characters in order to reach a point of compromise and unity.

Weaving personal conflict (influenced by tropes) into your story should enhance both the external and internal conflict arcs. Your cowboy (or musician or athlete or firefighter) will still be a cowboy at the end of the book, but the internal struggle that unfolds throughout the narrative should deliver him from an unfulfilled, less happy cowboy to a fulfilled cowboy who's found his happily ever after.

Relational conflict may arise from communication breakdowns, differing priorities, emotional baggage, and struggles to find common ground. The conflict should reflect the setting and dynamic of your characters. You may find this easier when combining character tropes that clash, though you can certainly throw a wrench in what would appear to be a totally compatible match. Look at the list of common traits, potential wounds, and even story world when considering where conflict may arise.

Does your career military hero scare the pants off the single mother heroine (okay . . . bad pun), who wants nothing more than stability and peace in her already baggage-ridden family? It can't be easy for the big-city lawyer and the small-town cowboy to see a future together, when it would mean one of them giving up everything they've ever worked for, can it? Ultimately, every couple must overcome their differences and make sacrifices to find their happy ending.

When pairing more complementary character tropes, you may have to go deeper into the wounds and vulnerabilities in order to find the source of conflict between characters, such as external pressures, societal expectations, mistakes or regrets of the past, physical danger, insecurities, and fears of long-term compatibility. You could also experiment with mixing tropes until you land on a combination that blows their compatibility to bits. That cinnamon roll hero may seem like the perfect guy to mend the broken heart of your grieving widow, but what happens when he also happens to be the best friend of her deceased husband. We'll tell you— turmoil ensues.

A NOTE FROM YOUR STORY COACH

Internal character tropes will almost always have internal conflict front and center. External character tropes can go either way, but certain categories such as emotional baggage tropes are more likely to lean toward a prominent internal conflict.

-JB

Regardless of whether your primary conflict is an internal struggle or external force, both must be integral to the plot of your romance. Will the conflict push your characters together or will it force them apart? Are your characters happy to be in such close proximity, or has this put a real damper on their plans to never associate with that person *ever*? Consider where you are in the plot structure (are they nearing the midpoint or the dark moment?) and how that should influence their current dynamic. And how have the events of your story challenged your character in ways that have led to a gradual or dramatic shift in their perspective, behavior, relationships, and beliefs?

By selecting and combining appropriate character tropes, authors can create a rich tapestry of conflicts that draw readers into the romance novel. Skillful execution allows for character growth, emotional tension, and resolution, all of which contribute to a compelling and engaging story.

CHAPTER 8

CHARACTER TROPES AND READER WISH FULFILLMENT

At the top of each trope or trope subsection, we've laid out what "reader desire" or "wish" the trope fulfills. This is hugely important in crafting a story that meets the reader's expectations and satisfies that deeper longing they carry with them into the story.

One of the biggest secrets to succeeding in the area of reader wish fulfillment is in nailing down the desires and fantasies of your target audience. Understand the preferences of your readers, their desires for content and expectations (as we've already noted, the content and even character expectations of steamy romance or erotica readers is going to differ greatly from the expectations and desires of clean or inspirational romance readers!) The reader desires and wishes that we refer to in encyclopedia entries tap into fundamental human experiences, emotions, and desires. There are many other areas where you may want to cast a wide net in pulling in readers— plot, conflict, characters—but if you focus on pleasing every reader, you won't *captivate* any of them. This is why genre and reading categories exist; some segregation ensures that readers who already know they love what you have to offer know where to find it.

Tropes can function in the same way—especially when you are intentional about satisfying reader wish fulfillment. Some character tropes are popular because we can relate to them (see **Nerd/Genius, Widow(er)**, **Single Parent**, or **Seasoned Characters**). The reader's desire these characters fulfill is that—despite our quirks, baggage, or history—we are wanted, loved, and accepted exactly as we are.

We gravitate toward other characters because we wish we knew them (see all of the Money, Money Tropes). These tropes fulfill the reader's desire to be secure and provided for, as well as adored and cherished beyond any material possession.

Some Characters are popular because they are so wildly different from our own reality that it is a fun escape (see **Pirate, Viking, Highlander**). These tropes feed the reader's desire for adventure, as well as to be deemed special by a larger-than-life hero.

Other Characters pull on our admiration for the qualities of the heroes (see **Men in Uniform, Doctor**). These tropes fulfill the reader's wish to be saved and protected by someone strong, noble, loyal, and competent.

There are others, but as you are writing, be cognizant of what deeper desire your reader might have for choosing to read this character. Even readers who read across sub-genres will have these desires, and these wish fulfillment strategies can be used to fulfill nearly any given reader desire regardless of the chosen trope. If the story aligns with a specific wish fulfillment, such as the desire to be loved and cherished above all else, you don't *need* to use a Billionaire to do it! Oftentimes, this is where the layering and mixing of tropes can add complexity and unexpected elements to your narrative and characters. With that being said, the reader desires we have pinpointed at the beginning of each encyclopedia entry are just the most obvious wish fulfilled by that Character.

Let the way that your hero interacts with your heroine fulfill that desire in her heart as well, and it will deeply resonate with your readers. This emotional connection between the reader and the love interest allows readers to empathize with the characters' challenges, victories and personal growth.

A NOTE FROM YOUR MARKETING COACH

When you know your audience, you can zero in on the romance themes, character traits, and scenarios that resonate with them, helping you select and adapt the character tropes or any other tropes you work into your story. Choose characters with personalities and values that appeal to your target audience and adapt tropes to more closely align with their expectations and desires.

-TGE

Because you want the reader to identify and empathize with the characters, you should create relationships based on mutual respect, communication, and growth. Readers appreciate seeing healthy dynamics and are much less likely to disengage from the romance narrative if they consider the relationship to be a positive example.

Another powerful tool for incorporating reader wish fulfillment is to allow your Character to influence subtext. These layers of meaning and unspoken emotions between characters create tension and a sense of immersion into the story. Unexpressed or hidden feelings and desires revealed to the reader through subtext can also create a sense of building intimacy and even anticipation. When the subtext finally becomes text (like when we watch the reformed heroine dance around the fact that she loves the leading man for chapters upon chapters until she finally confesses it aloud), the payoff feels richly rewarding.

Character tropes can both influence and enhance subtext, especially in situations where your character says or does something contrary to their nature. Based on the expectations and familiarity of your character trope, the reader should know that there's more to the story than what's on the page! Readers love to feel like they are intimately acquainted with your characters and like they're in on all the juiciest secrets, and subtext throws that door right open. Because subtext forces your reader to look closer, it also invites them into deeper connection with the characters. When coupled with internal dialogue and reflection, you can confirm the hidden meaning of previously utilized subtext to assure your reader they are on the right track or to reveal internal struggles and desires.

As a note, the greatest wish fulfillment your reader has come looking for, is that happily ever after. They want a glimpse into a world where love conquers all and broken people overcome challenges and hardships, making the happy ending well-earned and that much more satisfying.

Remember that while incorporating wish fulfillment can enhance your romance books, it's essential to maintain authenticity, well-rounded characters, and a compelling plot to avoid coming across as contrived or formulaic. Balancing reader desires with originality will help you to create meaningful and memorable stories.

CHAPTER 9

SUCCESSFUL USE OF CHARACTER TROPES

AVOIDING PITFALLS

Character tropes can go wrong in romance novels when they're executed in a way that feels formulaic, unrealistic, or extreme. Some of the most common pitfalls of character tropes include: lack of depth, unrealistic behavior, unhealthy dynamics, predictability, stereotypes, difficulty for characters to relate or empathize, and lack of growth. You can avoid these pitfalls by building on top of the framework and patterns provided by tropes to create complex characters, by subverting tropes, and by choosing character tropes for the love interest and side characters in such a way that it creates tension and pushes your main character toward the path of transformation.

We'll look at each of the ways character tropes tend to fall flat:

Lack of depth: If characters are one-dimensional and solely adhere to the trope, it can result in flat, uninteresting personalities that fail to engage readers. This also leads to caricature-like heroes and heroines and stereotypical characters. These stereotypes can lead to insensitive or offensive portrayals and very quickly turn off readers.

Unrealistic/inconsistent behavior: If your character's actions don't make sense based on their belief system, personal history, or current circumstances, it can make the story feel contrived, and conflict and resolutions feel convenient and unearned.

Unhealthy dynamics: Choosing stereotypical or "extreme" character tropes such as Alpha-hole, too-stupid-to-live, or damsel in *too much* distress opens the door to romanticizing or glorifying negative or immature behavior, perpetuating harmful ideals, and unhealthy relationships that readers find it difficult to root for (because they really shouldn't).

Predictability: When authors rely too heavily on tropes to carry their story, or when tropes are never subverted or given any unique twists/creative elements, the story often feels overly predictable and formulaic. This can lead readers to anticipate key moments and outcomes in your story and diminish reader investment in the journey of your characters.

Lack of growth: Readers have difficulty empathizing with static, unengaging character arcs. Not only will readers find it difficult to connect with a character who makes the same mistakes over and over without ever learning something from it, but they'll have little to no interest in rooting for their happily ever after.

Clichés: When mishandled, the use of common tropes can lack originality, seem like lazy writing, and be cliched. If you feel you don't have any fresh insight or creative contribution to a repetitive or oft-used trope, consider breaking into something new rather than falling back on the familiar. You could also try layering tropes from a different framework category or flipping a trope on its head.

Heavy-handed: If every last detail of your story from conflict to theme is dripping with the remnants of your character trope, it can feel like a bit *too* much for readers. Some character tropes like **Cowboy** and **Royalty** handle such a hostile takeover a little more smoothly, but others may benefit from the infusion of the unexpected crashing into their trope bubble.

To avoid these pitfalls, it's important to use tropes thoughtfully, adding unique elements to the characters and story that differentiate them from typical portrayals of your chosen trope. Balancing recognizable elements with unexpected twists and nuanced character development can help create a more compelling and memorable romance novel.

CHARACTER TROPE VS. CHARACTER'S CAREER

Some character tropes may be derived from occupations, but the two are not the equivalent. The character trope is centered around the motivations, goals, and personality of the character. Keep in mind, some character tropes have nothing to do with career (see *Internal Character Tropes* chapter and *Backstory and Emotional Baggage Tropes* chapter for examples).

Your character trope or the occupation of the protagonist needs to be present in the story, it does not need to dominate it. There must be a balance. If, for example, piracy or firefighting overshadow the romance, then it's no longer a romance. It's a pirate story or a firefighter action story with a romantic subplot. Find a balance where you include enough of your character trope to satisfy readers, but make sure that its inclusion is advancing the story and the romance arc. Keep in mind, if you could switch out your cowboy for a cop, or your athlete for an accountant, you haven't fulfilled the necessary elements of the character trope to satisfy your readers.

Don't make it too technical. Readers are coming for the romance. They may not be very knowledgeable about your character's career or industry. Any uncommon jargon needs to be explained in order to avoid confusing or turning off readers. Use simple language and get through the explanation quickly so that readers feel included without feeling inadequate. Do not dumb technical language down too much though, or your reader may feel patronized. Instead, consider that most are not experts, but that they have a general knowledge of the subject.

Certain tropes may blend seamlessly into the rest of your narrative, but oftentimes, authors try to force a trope into their story, or a trope that *theoretically* works ends up dragging down the narrative or distracting from the more central elements of the story. When this happens, sometimes it is a case of the *right* trope being employed the *wrong* way.

SUBVERTING EXPECTATIONS AND KEEPING TROPES FRESH

We wish that we could give you a list of all the ways your character trope can be flipped on its head or refreshed to take it from trite to tantalizing—but the truth is, if we did that, not only would it rid your story of the individuality that only you can bring, but soon enough, none of those creative methods would feel fresh, because we'd all be using them to stir up our stories! While some entries will include an idea to subvert reader expectations, most of them won't. The good news is that when you understand *why* these tropes are so beloved by readers and *how* they function, you'll be well-equipped to take and preserve all the yummy bits of your chosen trope and mix them in with unexpected theme, setting, or plot elements that will leave your readers in awe.

For any trope, you can generally freshen things up by:

- adding complexity to characters or flipping gender roles (the Prince in Peril rather than the Damsel in Distress)
- layering additional character tropes (internal or external) for one or both protagonists
- switching up settings or time periods (What happens when you take your Scottish Highlander and throw him in the American colonies? How does planting your pirate in the twenty-first century alter the trajectory of your narrative?)
- subverting expectations (unexpected twists that defy the usual trajectory of the trope like a billionaire who gives away nearly all of his earnings)
- exploring inner conflicts (using past experience and current circumstances, put the character's doubts, struggles, and growth in direct conflict with their values and trope characteristics)
- embracing diversity (exploring different cultures can change the entire lens through which you tell your story, and stories with central characters of color are in high-demand—just be sure to enlist the help of a sensitivity reader)
- highlighting your character's community (create strong secondary characters who will guide and challenge your character; utilize unconventional or unexpected friendships that will broaden the worldview of your trope-created characters)

- infusing humor and wit or introducing quirks (this goes a long way to giving your character a distinct personality and making them memorable)
- giving your characters unique interests, hobbies, or careers to influence their interactions, behavior, and relationship dynamics
- creating complex or unexpected backstories that challenge the stereotypes associated with your trope
- using the transformation arc of your character to highlight ways in which they have overcome challenges inherent to their trope or rejected a long-held belief that stemmed from the nature of their trope

You may also utilize humor and self-awareness mixed with a healthy dose of self-deprecation to acknowledge and play with some of the common conventions of your character trope—this allows your reader to laugh with the character rather than at them.

Remember, the goal is not to completely abandon the trope but to infuse it with unexpected elements and depth. You can retain the core appeal of your character trope while freshening it up with your own creativity and unique author voice. This approach can make your novel stand out while still resonating with readers who enjoy the familiar comfort of well-loved tropes.

CHAPTER 10

CHARACTER TROPES
AND "THE MARKET"

It's a common question in romance writing circles. ***How do I make my books more marketable?*** You'll find dozens of answers in the comments that all read the same: Add more tropes to your books!

While we are firm believers in tropes (obviously, we're writing this entire series of books about them), we also believe that tropifying your work isn't enough. Jessica writes all about this in her book *Beyond the Beats: Writing a Romance that Readers Can't Resist.* There is far more to a compelling and sellable romance than slapping a few tropes on the blurb and calling it a day.

However, it wouldn't have become advice if there wasn't a hint of truth in it. Tropes reign supreme in the romance genre. All tropes are powerful for marketing, don't get us wrong. But character tropes probably have the highest potential for marketing benefit, and we don't want you to miss out on that.

CHAPTER 10

So let's talk about the current (late 2023) romance market as it pertains to character tropes.

Reminder: We're talking generally about sweet, clean, or inspirational romance. If you write in other genres, the market will look quite different.

Here's what we know—Every author we've talked to will tell you that readers SAY they like or dislike one thing, but the sales say something different. You can decide which voice you want to listen to, but we think actions speak louder than words. So no matter how much readers claim to be tired of Billionaires and Cowboys, the sales and bestseller charts say something entirely different. Obviously there will always be some discrepancy in reader preference, but among the plethora of character tropes, we can see some general trends based on which ones sell like hot cakes regardless of how saturated the category is, which ones take all the heat, and which ones readers are begging for more of.

CHARACTER TROPES WITH A BAD RAP

Billionaire romances (or really any of the Money, Money character tropes) can be a hard sell (especially in Christian/Inspirational romance). Whether it's a perception of greed, materialism, or the "unrealistic" nature of these stories, readers find plenty of things to rag on when it comes to these tropes.

Alpha Males are definitely less popular in clean romance genres, though we think it is likely because they are conflated with the meaner/unkind Alpha-hole from steamy romance. So it's not that readers don't LIKE Alpha Male characters, as much as it is they don't think they are *supposed* to like them. While you're unlikely to sell a lot of copies of sweet romance with "Falling for her Alpha

Best Friend" style titles—if you write the story with an Alpha hero (meeting all the expectations of the Alpha trope with the help of this encyclopedia, of course), it's quite possible that readers will rave about him in the reviews.

Same goes for Billionaires or other rich characters—it seems shallow to admit you enjoy reading about the rich guy falling for the poor girl. But guilty pleasure sales are still sales.

MOST POPULAR TROPES

Billionaires (despite the flack they receive) continue to perform strongly in contemporary stories, while Regency handily dominates historical romance. Cowboys remain popular in every niche, and military heroes never seem to lose their appeal for readers. There are relatively strong niches for Athletes and Medical Professionals. Bad Boy tropes (including Mafia, even in clean and sweet) are also gaining popularity.

UNDERSERVED TROPES

Every reader poll we have ever seen shows that romance readers want more characters that are over the age of forty or even fifty. That makes the **Seasoned Character** trope one that is especially underserved. The adventure tropes (**Pirate**, **Highlander**, **Viking**) tend to be underserved in clean romance as well and readers wanting these tropes without steam struggle to find what they are looking for. The **Men in Uniform** trope tends to be dominated by **Military** heroes, but the others (**Firefighters** and **Law Enforcement**) don't have nearly as much competition.

To be clear, any character trope can make a marketable story. The question will be whether that character trope will be one that is the backbone of your marketing decisions.

COVERS, KEYWORDS, AND BLURBS . . . OH MY!

Once you've chosen a character trope to use as a tool for your marketing, then you have some decisions to make.

People use the phrase "writing to market" when they write a billionaire character because there is a big market for them. But truly "writing to market" means writing a billionaire book that *meets the expectations of* a billionaire book, a.k.a. actually writing the story to the billionaire market . . .

This entire book is about how to execute the decision you made when you chose to "write to market"—and how to do it successfully. Most of this book is about how to write to market within the actual words of the book and hitting the trope in the way readers are looking for. But we don't want to skip over the importance of "marketing to market" either.

A NOTE FROM YOUR MARKETING COACH

I recommend featuring your strongest marketing trope (Character or otherwise) somewhere in the title, subtitle, or series name. You don't need the word *cowboy* in all three places! If you can't think of any more Billionaire book titles, then maybe you only include it in the series name and have the traditional guy in a nice suit on the cover. Readers are smart. They'll figure it out.

-TGE

You are sending all kinds of signals to your reader with your title, subtitle, book cover, and blurb. Tara (the marketing coach at The Inspired Author) always recommends that research be step one in your decision-making process. What are others doing when they write this Character?

Do you want the word "Cowboy" in your title? Or can you convey the Character with a less obvious title by using the subtitle, cover image, or words like "ranch" or "creek" in the title? If you are writing a character trope to market, you need to communicate that to your readers before they even open the first page. Preferably before they even read the blurb, because character tropes are so important.

Whether you choose to use trope-laden titles like "Secret Marriage for Her Billionaire Best Friend" is up to you. We're not saying you should or shouldn't. The truth is, using the character trope in the title is often a very successful way to signal readers that it is a book they want, but they aren't necessarily the most intriguing or creative titles.

Let's break down Tara's current series of firefighter romances. Here is the info for the first book:

The One Who Got Away:

A Small-Town Christian Firefighter Romance

Second Chance Fire Station Book 1

See how many tropes are in there? We see at least three, and if you read the blurb, you'll see that there's also a bit of an **Actress/Celebrity** trope, though it wasn't especially emphasized in the story.

The main focus on tropes for marketing this series is that they are all 1) **Firefighters** in a 2) **Small Town**, and every single book is a 3) **Second Chance** romance. Each story has additional tropes, because no one wants to write (or read) the same story over and over! Other tropes included in

MARKET YOUR BOOK BASED ON THE READER WISH YOU ARE FULFILLING

this series are **Amnesia**, **Forbidden Romance**, **Redeemed Marriage**, and more . . . But the character trope is still the one that is front and center with the Firefighter on every cover.

You'll also want to include your best tropes (again, all four categories of framework tropes) in the keywords for your book.

There are some character tropes that impact the story, but you might not necessarily choose to feature them on the packaging of the book. You can lean into those character tropes (and the included reader wish fulfillment) in your ad copy, teasers, book trailers, or blog posts. Tropes like **Nerd/Genius**, **Widow(er)**, **Damsel in Distress**, or **Slacker** might be tropes that aren't obvious in the packaging. You can write a **Musician** character without having a guy with his guitar on the front—maybe you want the cover to focus on the **Small Town** trope instead! That just means people will have to read the blurb to know what they are getting, and it is up to you to make that decision based on what you want to communicate to your readers first.

Market your book based on the reader wish you are fulfilling. This is our last piece of marketing advice, and it makes sense because it brings this entire section full circle. In the rest of this book, we talk a lot about what "wish fulfillment" each trope provides. If you've written your story in such a way that it fulfills these reader wishes, then your only job when marketing is to let readers get a glimpse of that wish being fulfilled.

Sometimes, it is enough to simply communicate the trope to the reader. This is the lumberjack on the cover. The tailored black suit of a Billionaire. That might make them click and get to the blurb, but you still need to convince them. So how do you reel them in?

You need to go deeper than communicating the trope. Give them a taste of the wish they probably didn't even realize they were hoping would be met.

You need to signal to the reader that this isn't just a capital *P* Prince. This is a prince who would give up his kingdom if it meant saving his true love, which you can show in dialogue as he argues with his mom, the queen.

This isn't just a capital *S* Single Mom. This is a single mom who finds someone that embraces the role of fatherhood and grows to love her child as his own, seen from the mother's eyes as she watches him tuck her little girl into bed.

This isn't just any capital *B* Bodyguard. This is a bodyguard who sees the heroine as valuable and worth saving, not because she is a celebrity or because it is his job, but because he can't fight his feelings for her any longer.

It's the emotion, the promise that the character trope is making— that's what you need to communicate in your blurbs or TikToks or book trailers or teaser quote images or excerpts in your newsletter. And since you'll know all of those things ahead of time, you'll have dozens of quotes and excerpts to choose from that are perfect for hitting the mark.

Without further ado . . . let's see those character tropes!

Part Three

THE CHARACTER
TROPE ENCYCLOPEDIA

CHAPTER 11

INTERNAL CHARACTER TROPES

Each of the internal character tropes in this chapter is derived from some of the most popular literary archetypes in fiction. They will carry elements of the universal symbolism, themes, and patterns that have transcended both time and history.

Archetypes are deeply rooted in the human experience, universal motivations, and emotions, meaning they will resonate deeply with readers when done well and can have a significant emotional impact. Some of the most basic archetypes include the hero, the villain, the best friend, and the mentor.

Because genre fiction carries its own constraints on story structure and development, we have adapted what we consider to be the most relevant fiction archetypes for use in our internal character tropes chapter. You might consider the distinction to be that while archetypes are universal and transcendent, character tropes aren't necessarily lasting. But they are recognizable and they will appear frequently in a particular genre of storytelling. It's somewhat narrower than the scope of archetypes, because they are used to quickly establish certain characteristics and roles for characters and to define these characters within the context of their given genre (romance).

The tropes discussed in this section will be addressed separately, as they are vastly different in nature, expectations, strengths, and pitfalls. However, each one hearkens back to an original archetype and is rooted firmly in the human condition, making them some of the deepest and most relatable tropes.

ALPHA MALE

BAD BOYS

CINNAMON ROLL

DAMSEL IN DISTRESS

ECCENTRIC

THE GRUMP

LONE WOLF/RECLUSE

RAGS TO RICHES/LOSS HEIR(ESS)

ALPHA MALE

THESE HEROES FEED THE READER'S DESIRE TO BE PURSUED WITH UNWAVERING PASSION

In these stories, the hero is a strong and dominant figure, typically displaying traditionally masculine characteristics. The Alpha hero is, above all else, a leader, and he commands respect (overtly or unconsciously). He is used to being in control of the situation and in control of himself. His competence and ability entice others to follow him, but they don't always earn him respect.

He doesn't apologize for who he is or what he wants—whether that comes through as confidence or cockiness.

A good Alpha Male is unselfish and leads with integrity, caring about those in his charge and leading with a strong moral compass. He will often put his own desires on the back burner in order to show up for those under his charge. This may not be the case at the beginning of your story, but if not, it should be part of your protagonist's character arc, and it ultimately *should* be where your alpha male ends the story.

Your character may actually start out the story in this way, but their circumstances cause them to falter. In that case, they should return to this type of healthy leadership and dominance through their transformation arc, and often with a less-than-subtle push from the love interest.

Regardless of the conflict introduced throughout the course of your novel, your alpha male will face these challenges by drawing upon his inner strength and pushing through to the happily ever after.

The right Alpha Male will make your reader's heart beat faster and their stomach flutter. Flawed but honorable, his flaws should pull the heroine (and the reader) in, making them desperate to know more about this crack in the armor. But even with his flaw, an Alpha Male will act honorably—though that code of honor might be his own or dependent on the culture he is part of.

WHY READERS LOVE IT

One of the key reasons readers love Alpha Males is their inherent impressiveness. These characters are larger than life, possessing a certain magnetism that commands attention and admiration. Yet, beneath their tough exterior lies a fascinating complexity that captivates readers. Despite their unwavering strength, Alpha Males are, at their core, human. The struggle with vulnerability and the battle between their emotions and stoic facade allows readers to connect with them on a profound level. Revealing even a hint of humility becomes a potent tool to generate empathy, forging an emotional bond between readers and these intriguing characters.

As the story unfolds, the Alpha Male's evolution plays a pivotal role in capturing the hearts of readers. Initially resistant to revealing their more vulnerable side, they gradually open up to the heroine, unveiling the depths of their emotions. This journey of emotional growth and increasing vulnerability will not come easy to the Alpha Male, and this struggle keeps readers on the edge of their seats.

Moreover, Alpha males are unapologetically assertive in expressing their desires and pursuing what they want. Readers are enticed by their fearless determination and unwavering pursuit of their heart's desire. When the object of their affection is the strong-willed and independent heroine, such a clash of wills creates a tantalizing dynamic, further fueling readers' interest.

The emotional intensity displayed by Alpha Males is another factor in leaving readers swooning. Their strength and passion extend not only to physical prowess but also to their unyielding commitment to the love interest. This level of devotion creates an all-encompassing love story that resonates deeply with readers, pulling them into a world where the power of love knows no bounds.

Additionally, Alpha males offer a sense of safety and security that appeals to readers' primal instincts. Their fiercely protective nature ensures that the heroine feels cherished and sheltered in their presence. In a world full of uncertainties, the unwavering dedication of an Alpha Male serves as a beacon of stability.

READER EXPECTATIONS

Readers who love a good Alpha Male are looking for the strong, confident leader discussed above. Give him plenty of opportunities to show his leadership, and don't be afraid to use side character interactions to give context as to how he operates and what he values.

But that character can't be perfect, and his circumstances tend to be high stakes. Common internal conflicts for these characters drive the narrative forward and force him to make decisions that show him who he is: truth vs loyalty, ambition vs relationship, power vs abuse, confidence vs insecurity.

Your heroine should not be weak or overshadowed by your Alpha hero but should to stand her own, challenging him and pushing him to reach his highest potential.

We should understand the hero's persistence at pursuing her and his dedication to winning her heart—because that's just what it should be. Remember that your alpha male knows what he wants, and he works hard to get it. Being pursued (in a loving, not-stalkerish way) is the reader wish these heroes were created to fulfill.

Whatever your alpha's goal is, your reader should understand *why* he wants it. These characters do not tend to be impulsive, and without understanding their motivation, their actions may not come across in the best light. With the proper motivation, your reader is able to empathize with your alpha hero, even when his actions seem brash or abrasive.

Alpha Male heroes are one trope where it is more than okay to lean into the physical appeal of your hero. We're pretty adamant that an Alpha Male should be attractive. He should make the reader and the heroine weak in the knees—average guys just don't have that effect, and they typically don't have the innate confidence that eventually grows into a full-blown Alpha Male character.

COMMON PITFALLS

The heroine as your alpha male's only weakness: These characters are honorable and impressive, but they are also flawed. Give them at least one weakness, beyond the mere presence of your female main character in their lives. Your character's vulnerability will endear him to the reader and his love interest.

Alpha-hole: Your alpha male is bound to have a strong personality, and depending on the characteristics of your heroine, he may come off as something of a jerk. However, he should not be a bully or overtly disrespectful, or your reader may not be able to forgive him for his less-than-pleasant demeanor in the beginning. He may be persistent in his pursuits, but he should not *always* be a jerk about it.

Common character traits of an *Alpha-hole* include: controlling, possessive, volatile, jealous, manipulative, cruel. There is a fine line between Alpha and Alpha-hole, so tread lightly if you are not intentionally writing this darker twist on an Alpha character.

COMMONLY PAIRED TROPES

The Alpha Male pairs well with any of the *Money, Money* tropes such as Billionaire, Athlete, and Celebrity/Musician. This is because the majority of these career tropes require a certain tenacity and passion that comes easily to Alphas. For this same reason, you may see Alpha Males in certain *Passion and Competence* character tropes, Boss/Employee relationships, or Workplace settings as well.

The cultural environment of tropes such as Highlander, Viking, and Pirate also place a high value on Alpha-type heroes, making these a common combination.

The power combo of the Alpha Male with the Bad Boy creates a complexity and contradiction in your hero that has proven to be incredibly popular with some readers. While this alpha male is still confident and assertive, they may lack some of the steadfast control of other Alpha heroes, instead leaning toward impulsivity and rebellion. The contrast of these characteristics leads to intense character growth and generates tension as well as some degree of mystery.

ALPHA MALE

Finally, the determination and relentlessness of Alpha Males sometimes lends itself to tropes such as Hidden Motives, Enemies to Lovers, Bodyguard, or Military. Stories where the Alpha Male is pursuing something aggressively (in addition to the heroine) give ample opportunity for his assertive and self-assured nature to shine.

POTENTIAL WOUNDS

Failing to do the right thing
Poor judgment leading to unintended consequences
Being forced to keep a dark secret
A toxic relationship
Finding out he was adopted
Infidelity
Misplaced loyalty
A parent's abandonment or rejection
Death of a parent
Growing up in a dangerous environment

COMMON TRAITS

Assertive	Protective	Authoritative
Competent	Decisive	Resilient
Commanding	Dominant	Self-assured
Intimidating	Strong	Courageous
Confident	Charismatic	Ambitious

BAD BOYS

THESE TROPES FEED THE READER'S DESIRE TO SEE THAT LOVE CAN AND DOES REDEEM THE BROKEN

BAD BOY/REBEL

REFORMED BAD BOY

PLAYBOY/RAKE/FLIRT

SLACKER

BAD BOY/REBEL

THIS TROPE FEEDS THE READER'S DESIRE TO BREAK FREE FROM SOCIETAL NORMS AND EXPECTATIONS

The Bad Boy/Rebel in romance novels is an alluring character trope. With a rebellious charm and air of mystery, he defies societal norms, drawing the heroine and readers into his world of excitement and unpredictability. His passion for life and experience evokes a strong reaction from readers, allowing them to be immersed in the highs and lows of the narrative drama.

At first glance, the Bad Boy appears to be a rule-breaker, someone who defies societal norms and rebels against authority. His disregard for conventional expectations makes him an intriguing figure. But the Bad Boy has a line that he *will not* cross, even if he will never tell what those boundaries are—and he is sure to make it clear that no one else will draw that line for him. This nonconformity serves as a stark contrast to more predictable and conventional suitors vying for the heroine's affection.

Despite the sometimes "poor reputation" or dalliances a Bad Boy character may be known for, he is far more than a Casanova. Beneath the tough exterior lies a complex character with emotional scars and hidden vulnerability, making him an enigmatic figure worth unraveling. His unyielding self-confidence and adventurous spirit lead the heroine on daring escapades and ignite a passionate connection.

These characters ooze charisma, despite frequently butting heads with others. When your bad boy does form a connection with others (like your heroine), the dynamics will likely involve shared challenges, banter, and being pushed out of their comfort zone, making these stories rife with chemistry and off-the-charts tension.

Your bad boy may lend himself to more intense or risky external obstacles and internal struggles that force the characters to grow and affect the trajectory of the romance arc. As the story unfolds, the Bad Boy's transformation becomes central, fueled by the heroine's love and support. True emotional intimacy may not come easily to your bad boy, and it will be important to allow your characters to open up to each other in order to deepen the relationship. This redemptive journey showcases the power of love to heal and captivate, despite the challenges posed by his impulsive nature.

For the sake of simplicity, we will refer to the Bad Boy as he—but this trope can absolutely be filled by a rebellious female. For an example of the Rebel Girl trope (and an unconventional pairing), check out the case study for *10 Things I Hate About You*.

WHY READERS LOVE IT

The Bad Boy trope can be summed up in one word: temptation. These characters have bad news written all over them, and yet heroines and readers alike can't resist a well-written Bad Boy. He is everything you shouldn't want . . . but you do anyway.

The allure of the Bad Boy lies in his unpredictability; readers are drawn to the uncertainty of his actions and the excitement of being swept away on an adventure with a man who lives life on the edge.

Beneath his tough exterior, the Bad Boy often carries emotional wounds or a troubled past, adding a layer of depth and vulnerability to his character. This duality of strength and sensitivity creates a complex persona that readers yearn to explore. Unraveling the layers of his personality and understanding the reasons behind his rebellious behavior becomes a tantalizing journey for readers, fostering a deeper emotional connection to the story.

There is some degree of risk in fraternizing with nearly every Bad Boy, making the romance oh so compelling and somewhat suspenseful—what will it cost your heroine to love this man? Most of us never actually want to fall for the Bad Boy, but there *is* something to the intensity and adventure of reading about someone else falling for him.

Moreover, the Bad Boy exudes an undeniable self-confidence and unapologetic authenticity that captures readers' attention. He doesn't seek validation from others, and his unwavering belief in himself is alluring. This self-assuredness acts as a powerful magnet, drawing the heroine—and by extension, the readers—toward him. But it is the very self-assuredness he portrays that eventually requires him to be vulnerable with the heroine. Seeing the man behind the reputation is what drives this story and keeps readers coming back.

Possibly the most important aspect of any Bad Boy trope, is the redemption arc. Readers love to see the Bad Boy be redeemed and learn to truly love. Seeing the transformation from a rough-and-tumble personality to someone capable of true love leaves the reader with a deeply satisfying sense of hope and optimism.

READER EXPECTATIONS

In Bad Boy romances, readers crave more than just a label. They want a character who embodies the essence of rebellion and adventure, a multifaceted soul whose motivations and desires are unveiled layer by layer. Instead of merely telling the reader that he is a Bad Boy, you must draw readers deep into his mind and heart and show us why he behaves this way.

His actions may be fueled by a thirst for adventure, an insatiable appetite for rebellion against the constraints of society, or perhaps even an ulterior motive beneath the facade of his outrageous behavior. By delving into the *why* behind his actions, you should uncover the driving forces that shape his character in the face of seemingly insurmountable obstacles.

In order for readers to sympathize with your hero, they must understand his motivations. This is where the past trauma, backstory, and deep-seated wound come in. These elements tend to involve difficult and uncomfortable topics, which a vast majority of readers love to see handled deftly in fiction.

Truly, the allure of the Bad Boy extends beyond his daring exploits. It is his troubled past, the scars etched on his soul, and his personal struggles that draw readers deeper into his story. As readers discover his past, they come to understand the reasons behind his seemingly reckless behavior, forging a profound connection with him and paving the way for a redemptive arc that resonates deeply.

The redemptive journey of the Bad Boy is of paramount importance, as readers anticipate witnessing his transformation into a better version of himself. Rooting for his redemption, readers find solace in knowing that love can heal even the most broken of souls. The growth and positive change that stem from his love for the heroine are pivotal, shaping the trajectory of the story. Yet be careful not to hand this redemption over too easily. While the heroine may serve as a catalyst or a helper in the spiritual journey of the hero, she can't be the ultimate solution.

Your bad boy *must* have a plausible and relevant motivation to change, and it should come from within himself. In Christian or inspirational romances, it's worth noting that the Bad Boy should absolutely be saved by Christ, and Christ alone, in order to satisfy reader expectations. It's his salvation in Christ that allows him to finally be able to form a loving and lasting relationship with the heroine.

In non-inspirational romances, authors can avoid this by making sure that the Bad Boy is changing for his own betterment rather than the benefit of someone else.

As the walls around his heart begin to crumble, you must be sure that the heroine—and readers—get a glimpse into the true essence of his emotional depth. This increasing vulnerability not only strengthens the connection between the characters but also showcases his growth as he learns to trust, love, and embrace the transformative power of a genuine and profound bond.

COMMON PITFALLS

Glorifying or normalizing toxic behavior: Your hero may struggle some with effective communication, but this doesn't give you the excuse to use toxic relationship dynamics, manipulation, or other problematic methods of communication and conflict resolution. This is where it becomes very easy to dislike the Bad Boy.

Approach with caution: Avoid crossing boundaries such as lack of consent or pushing the female character (or side characters) too hard to do anything they are resistant to. Your bad boy must respect his lady (and she should respect him too). Although he is bound to cross boundaries in virtually every other area of his life, choose wisely which boundaries he will trample over when it comes to the intimate relationship with the love interest, and make sure that he has a *believable* way back to her good side and respect. Your female character should make him work for any boundaries crossed—she is not a doormat and she should expect respect from him.

Shallow characterization/weak backstory: Creating a well-rounded character is absolutely critical for this trope. Give them a compelling backstory that explains their tough exterior and provides insight into their motivations and vulnerabilities. This humanizes them and makes them relatable to readers.

Weak redemption arc: Their transformation arc should be meaningful and lead to a satisfying resolution. The change will not be convincing if the reader (or any of the characters) believe that he was saved/redeemed by the love interest. Being saved by the heroine or any other external factor will feel shallow and underdeveloped.

COMMONLY PAIRED TROPES

Heroes in common Bad Boy environments include Athletes, Musicians/Celebrities, and even Billionaires—really any of the *Money, Money* tropes. As they say . . . more money, more problems. And what could be a better set up for your bad boy than that?

The power combo of the Alpha Male with the Bad Boy creates a complexity and contradiction in your hero that has proven to be incredibly popular with some readers. While this alpha male is still confident and assertive, he may lack some of the steadfast control of other Alpha heroes, instead leaning toward impulsivity and rebellion. The contrast of these characteristics leads to intense character growth and generates tension as well as some degree of mystery.

Tropes like Enemies to Lovers and Opposites Attract give opportunities for the contrast between the characters to add a delicious tension. Pairing the Bad Boy trope with the Good Girl or the Girl Next Door is almost too overdone, but that doesn't mean that it can't be done well. Of course, the Bad Boy represents a sense of adventure and radical change in the Good Girl's life, while she offers something of stability and a moral compass. It pairs well with the themes of redemption and forgiveness that are so common in Bad Boy stories.

Tropes that force them together such as Hidden Motives and Fake Relationship give strong adhesion, especially necessary if your heroine normally wouldn't associate with such a character.

Tropes like Hidden/Mistaken Identity and Hidden Motives are also strong because they naturally fit the tendency of the rebellious character to bend the rules to accomplish their goals.

As far as settings go, Bad Boy romances are common in Regency and Royalty romance, where the behavior of the rebel is especially contrary to the expectations placed upon him.

POTENTIAL WOUNDS

Failing at school
Failing to do the right thing
Poor judgement leading to unintended consequences
Being falsely accused of a crime
Being disowned
An abusive parent
Neglectful parents
Not being a priority for his parents

CHARACTER TRAITS

Rebellious	Irresistible	Confident
Mysterious	Risk taking	Charming
Defiant	Edgy	Independent
Nonconformist	Unpredictable	Adventurous
Daring	Self deprecating	Unconventional

REFORMED BAD BOY

*THIS TROPE FEEDS THE READER'S
DESIRE TO EXPERIENCE THE
HEALING POWER OF SECOND
CHANCES*

This hero carries the burden of a troubled past. The central thread of his transformation arc follows his effort to prove his redemption through his love for the other protagonist.

Although this character has already reformed prior to the beginning of your novel, he likely still carries shame, avoids triggers or reminders of his old life, has something to run from or hide from, and lives in fear of slipping back into the person he used to be. Deep down, the Reformed Bad Boy typically feels unworthy of being loved because of his past mistakes.

His reputation likely follows him, despite the changes he's made. Because of this, these heroes are often somewhat aloof or closed off; sometimes they have even maintained their antagonistic streak. This hero may be actively working to redeem his reputation, or he may continue letting people assume the worst about him (because, in some way, he still believes it is the truth). It is common for this story to feature secrets or decisions from the past coming back to haunt this character in some way—forcing him to face his past, and sometimes, for the love interest to discover new depths of the hero. This allows the Reformed Bad Boy to be fully known by his partner and realize that he is fully loved despite his past mistakes.

WHY READERS LOVE IT

As much as readers love to see the Bad Boy's original redemption story, they also love to relish in his changed heart and see him achieve a true and lasting happily ever after. The empathy and forgiveness that the reformed character likely still struggles to accept from others and himself sets up an emotionally rich and compelling love story.

As discussed in the previous section, Bad Boys are nuanced, multi-dimensional characters, and they have strengths and weaknesses just like the rest of us. While the reformed character has likely learned to appreciate and enhance his strengths for his own benefit and that of others, he may still struggle against old demons and bad habits from the past. The inner struggle of these characters trying to live as a new person and overcome past mistakes adds to the emotional depth of the story and engages readers' empathy.

There is a nearly universal appreciation for second chances. Second Chance stories always resonate with readers who believe in the power of personal change and new beginnings.

READER EXPECTATIONS

Reformed Bad Boy romances include many of the same elements as Bad Boy stories including: multifaceted heroes, thirst for adventure, sympathetic heroes, difficult/uncomfortable topics and the redemption arc. While this Bad Boy has mostly moved on from his from wayward life, he has yet to genuinely embrace this new identity. His feelings of unworthiness keep him from fully shedding the Bad Boy he used to be, especially when it comes to finding love. The process of truly accepting the new man he has become typically creates the redemption arc in these stories.

One of the most compelling ways to write these heroes is to cloak their past in a shroud of secrecy (and often shame). Because these heroes are their own worst critics, by the time their past mistakes are revealed in their full weight, most readers will already have fallen in love with the meek and humble spirit of your reformed hero.

These heroes may still struggle against societal norms and they will almost certainly retain their thrill-seeking tendencies, but in most cases, they will have developed healthier coping mechanisms that are less likely to be a detriment to themselves and their relationships. Rather than exploring the motivation behind negative actions (as you would with a bad, Bad Boy), authors should show that these characters are paralyzed by the fear and knowledge of who they are capable of being, often resulting in inaction in the face of challenges.

While the dark moment story of a Bad Boy romance has resulted in a character who conducts themselves with no regard for his own consequences or the consequences to those around him, the reformed hero is painfully aware of the consequences of his actions, whether they are isolated to his own life or the lives of others. Until this hero can accept himself for who is today, and not who he used to be, he will not be able to embrace the love of the heroine.

COMMON PITFALLS

Perpetuating stereotypes: Be careful that your Reformed Bad Boy does not fall into the trap of stereotypes. While the tall, dark, and handsome Bad Boy may still make your reader's heart flutter, he doesn't need to be manipulative, narcissistic, or an outright psychopath.

Convenient or cliched redemption: Just as we have to believe the reason for the Bad Boy transformation arc, we have to believe whatever the cause was for the Reformed Bad Boy to have changed his course prior to the events of the story.

Cardboard cutout: The Reformed Bad Boy can't lose everything unique and interesting in personality once the "bad boy" disappears. Be sure he has compelling motivations, quirks, and traits beyond the type of man he used to be. If your character lacks personality, it will not only bore your readers, it will feel inauthentic.

Lack of consequences: This is the former bank robber who got away miraculously and was never found out, never having to fess up or atone for his crimes, then he falls in love with the beautiful maiden . . . who just so happens to be the banker's daughter. Don't let your hero completely escape any kind of justice or consequence for his mistakes. Depending on the gravity of what he has done, he should at the very least struggle deeply under the weight of what his actions, if he hasn't already atoned for them in other ways.

I had to do it: The Reformed Bad Boy changed his ways because he saw the error in them. Don't minimize the choices he made back then or justify them too easily. If he were in the same situation now, he would likely do things differently. Give your character some introspective qualities and allow him to recognize that—even if his actions were based on a lie he believed or there were noble intentions hidden behind the rebellion—his choices have negative consequences for himself and others.

COMMONLY PAIRED TROPES

There is likely no more common pairing for the Reformed Bad Boy than a Second Chance romance. This trope allows the Reformed

Bad Boy to accept the forgiveness from the person he believes least likely to offer it.

Another common pairing includes Counselor/Pastor, leaning into the idea that a character has grown so far as to embrace a calling where he is helping others with their own identity and struggles, though he will still wrestle with his past.

Because the Reformed Bad Boy is often forced to face the sins of his past, tropes like Coming Home, Secret Baby, or Secret Marriage are solid options for those confrontations to take place.

POTENTIAL WOUNDS

Poor judgement leading to unintended consequences
Watching someone die
A life-threatening accident
Making a very public mistake
Public humiliation
Telling the truth but not being believed

COMMON TRAITS

Adventurous	Growing	Determined
Regretful	Compassionate	Sincere
Reflective	Resolute	Caring
Self deprecating	Empathetic	Transformed
Redeemed	Thoughtful	Feels unworthy

PLAYBOY/CHARMER

THIS TROPE FEEDS THE READER'S DESIRE TO BE PURSUED BY A HERO WHO COULD HAVE ANYONE HE WANTS

This trope may be referred to as the Playboy, Rake, Player, Flirt, or Charmer. It typically refers to a male character who is attractive, charming, confident (even arrogant), and has a reputation for promiscuity, flirtatious behavior, or dalliances. However, it is important to note that the reputation of these characters does not always reflect the true nature of their relationships or personality. Regardless of their conduct, the key to these characters is that they are desired by many, and they are known to make others feel desired.

The Playboy or Rake often indulges in casual relationships without any thought of long-term commitment. This cavalier attitude stems from a combination of his self-assured demeanor and past experiences, which may have shaped his belief in avoiding emotional entanglements.

They often undergo a transformation when they meet someone who makes them consider a more serious commitment, leading not only to a change in their romantic behavior but personal growth. While it is often the heroine that motivates the rake to reevaluate his attitude about relationships, the transformation must be rooted deeply in his own self-awareness.

Prior to this breakthrough, the Playboy will never willingly engage in the depths of love or pain. Instead, he cruises through life with the confidence and understanding that he can make nearly anyone bend to his will—leading to an existence that is satisfying on the surface, but incredibly lonely upon closer inspection.

WHY READERS LOVE IT

As much as his promiscuity is a glaring blemish on his point chart, there is no denying that rakish heroes make readers swoon. Their ability to navigate social situations with ease and captivate others through their charisma creates an engaging and intriguing dynamic. Highlight your hero's magnetic charm and wit, and your reader will easily understand why women are drawn to him.

Not to mention the sizzling chemistry between the couples in these stories. Because their dynamic is a central focus of the story, the intensity and passion of their connection easily captivates readers' hearts.

Because of the strong and sometimes manipulative personality of these heroes, they tend to be paired with confident and independent heroines. Readers love to see sparks fly as his attempts to charm the love interest only cause her to push him harder to confront his own flaws. Such interactions often lead to personal growth of both characters, but they also provide ample opportunities to inject wit and banter into the romance.

READER EXPECTATIONS

Like any other Bad Boy trope, these heroes should be layered with complexity—it is important to explore their motivations, fears, and any wounds that may shape this behavior. These nuances of character, especially when revealing his vulnerability, will make him more relatable and interesting. Not only this, but it should give readers an understanding of the reasons behind his flirtatious behavior. The hero's past relationships, experiences, or trauma should evoke empathy in the reader, allowing them to connect with his struggles. While your hero might have a reputation as a rake, that's not all he is.

To garner readers' support for his personal growth, infuse your hero with redeemable qualities, characteristics, or hidden depths that inspire rooting for his transformation and ultimate success. For this reason, it's common to see a bromance (or meaningful male friendship) in these stories as a way to point toward character development outside of the Rake's romantic relationships. These friendships highlight his positive qualities and provide opportunities for humor through wit, teasing, and a few well-timed jokes.

As the hero starts to fall for the love interest, he will find it difficult to break free of the identity he has created for himself. He may not even recognize the genuineness of his affections, being so confused with playing the role of the suave and seductive suitor that he doesn't notice the pain he inflicts on the heroine with his unwillingness to embrace intimacy. This should provide obstacles that the hero must overcome on his path to change, ensuring a satisfying and meaningful resolution to both his personal character arc and the romance arc.

COMMON PITFALLS

Shallow stereotypes: Avoid reducing the Playboy character to a one-dimensional stereotype. While their charm and flirtatiousness are defining traits, ensure that they have depth, complexity, and motivations beyond their seductive persona. Let the reader into your hero's internal struggles as he grapples with his feelings for the heroine and his desire to change.

Unrealistic transformation: Be cautious not to rush the transformation of the Playboy character too quickly or unrealistically. Their change from a carefree player to someone considering commitment should be gradual and well-founded, reflecting genuine personal growth. Sudden shifts in behavior, such as abruptly abandoning their flirtatious tendencies without proper development, can feel forced and undermine their credibility.

Superficial redemption: Don't rely solely on the romantic interest to be the catalyst for change. While their relationship can prompt change, ensure that the Playboy's growth is driven by his internal struggles and desire for personal betterment. Develop internal motivations and triggers that prompt the Playboy to reevaluate his lifestyle and choices and show how his transformation impacts his relationships with friends, family, and colleagues. Failing to explore the Playboy's vulnerabilities and fears can make him seem distant and unrelatable. Glimpses into his insecurities provide depth and allow readers to connect emotionally with his journey.

Lack of respect or consent/too much manipulation: Excessive charm can easily slip into manipulation. It is important to demonstrate the hero's respect and admiration for the love interest, outside of her physical beauty. Ensure that the Playboy's flirtatious behavior respects consent and boundaries. Avoid glorifying non-consensual actions or objectification, as this can perpetuate harmful narratives.

Ignoring consequences: Address the consequences of the Playboy's past actions. Ignoring the impact of his flirtatious behavior on others can undermine the authenticity of his growth and the stakes of his transformation.

Lack of emotional intimacy with heroine: Because it is the emotional intimacy of commitment that this hero has avoided through most of his romantic history, it is imperative that he is willing to show more vulnerability and emotional depth as the relationship progresses.

COMMONLY PAIRED TROPES

Playboys are common in many of the Money, Money tropes, including Athletes, Musicians/Celebrities, and Billionaires. The easy access to money and fame makes the currency of affection and physical intimacy an alluring outlet for characters who have their other needs easily met.

The charismatic Rake can also be paired with a Slacker character, giving the slacker a singular focus on the attention of the women he pursues.

Like the Rebel, the Rake is especially prominent in Regency or Royalty romance, where his behavior is especially unsavory compared to the expectations of the society. However, these flirtatious bad boys are also popular in other settings.

POTENTIAL WOUNDS

Infidelity
Choosing not to be involved in a child's life
Poor judgement leading to unintended consequences
Being the victim of a vicious rumor
Being abandoned or rejected by a parent
A parent's divorce

BAD BOYS

The death of a parent
Public failure
Parents who loved conditionally

COMMON TRAITS

Charismatic	Witty	Unpredictable
Charming	Self assured	Nonchalant
Confident	Seductive	Irresistible
Flirtatious	Playful	Adventurous
Carefree	Reckless	Spirited

SLACKER

THIS TROPE FEEDS THE READER'S DESIRE TO SEE LOVE BRING OUT THE PASSION AND POTENTIAL OF THEIR PARTNER.

This trope portrays a typically male character (though the role could easily be filled by a female) who is easygoing, challenges convention and is especially quick-witted or humorous. When humor is an especially prominent characteristic, the Slacker may also be identified as the Class Clown trope, but sometimes the Slacker is just known for his wit, sarcasm, or sardonic quips. They tend to use humor and their lack of desire for any meaningful endeavors as a defense mechanism. To those who love and care for the Slacker, their devil-may-care attitude is both endearing and incredibly frustrating, and though they may try to encourage them toward more worthy pursuits, they are rarely successful.

Their tendency to put things off or take the path of least resistance, as well as their aversion to anything serious often extends to relationships, making them hesitant to commit. Nonetheless, these characters are often seen as the lovable jerk—the guy who drives everyone nuts, and yet you just can't seem to stay mad at him. When paired with a rigid or extremely disciplined love interest or side character, they are likely to exert their influence, eventually getting others to act more spontaneously or let loose.

This hero is all about the long game. He'll take a few good blows in battle, so long as he's the victor at the end of the war. His boldness often presents as going out on a limb with a cheesy pickup line or pushing his teasing too far—but the resulting rejection doesn't sway his confidence. This makes him somewhat more open to revealing vulnerabilities and letting down his guard with the love interest, because he mistakenly believes that he will never lose control of his faculties, and he will always come out on top.

The Slacker often possesses many hidden talents and redeemable qualities, making them intriguing and constantly keeping the reader on the edge of their seats. It is not uncommon for these characters to be secret geniuses or possess some other extraordinary talent that they prefer to keep hidden for the sake of keeping everyone's expectations low. Seeing these characters embrace their strengths and come into their true potential is a joy for readers.

WHY READERS LOVE IT

In a romance story, the Class Clown or Slacker hero's interaction with the love interest often leads to transformative character development and a deeper exploration of their motivations and vulnerabilities. The contrast between their carefree exterior and their potential for more creates an incredibly compelling dynamic that easily draws readers in.

Goofy heroes infuse humor into the story, adding moments of laughter and entertainment that make the reading experience enjoyable. The inherent humor of these characters can serve as a valuable tool for diffusing tense moments, promoting open communication between characters, and even resolving conflicts, giving the story an uplifting and usually lighthearted tone. At the same time, their penchant for humor can create opportunities for unexpected challenges, misunderstandings, and tension. There's nothing like some poorly timed hijinks to land our lovers in a simmering pot of hot water . . . and we all know what happens when you turn up the heat.

One of the appeals of these characters are that they sometimes feel infinitely more relatable than larger-than-life billionaires and basically perfect royals or cinnamon rolls. The insecurities, doubts, and self-deprecation of these characters makes them extremely relatable. Allowing the reader to connect at such a basic human level quickly hooks readers and keeps them invested in the personal and romantic journey.

READER EXPECTATIONS

The Slacker's charisma and ability to make others laugh will either serve as an initial attraction for the protagonist or love interest, sparking interest and curiosity—or else it will be a total turn off.

In either case, his charm will prove difficult for the heroine to resist. The easy smile and twinkle in this hero's eye makes it easy for him to establish rapport and forge connections with others. Be sure to give your hero a distinctive style of humor that sets him apart. He could be witty, sarcastic, or use physical comedy, but ensure the humor aligns with his personality.

As the romance develops, you should give this character moments of vulnerability when he drops the funny-man act, allowing for a glimpse of the real person beneath the facade. This adds depth to the relationship, but it also highlights the uniqueness and genuineness of their connection. This could involve shared interests, past experiences, or even a clash of personalities that leads to irresistible chemistry.

In order to do this, you should strike a balance between his humorous moments and moments of depth. This will ultimately make him more well-rounded and compelling as a romantic lead. Introduce challenges that go beyond humor, allowing the Slacker to confront deeper issues that require emotional growth and maturity.

While these heroes may not readily seek out responsibility, they should be given the opportunity to rise to the occasion, allowing them to demonstrate their unexpected strengths and skill. The journey of these reluctant heroes should involve learning to balance their playful nature with being serious, reliable and trustworthy when needed. Beneath their carefree demeanor, there is a man (or woman) who truly desires to show up for those that they love and care about.

COMMON PITFALLS

Lack of depth: If the hero's humor overshadows other aspects of his personality, it makes them seem one-dimensional or lacking in emotional depth. It's not uncommon to see authors address the fact that the Slacker uses his humor and wit as a defense mechanism without really exploring why. Is it to mask his vulnerabilities, deal with personal challenges, or connect with others? Show the reader that he's more than just a funny guy.

Mismatched tone: In stories with emotional or intense themes, a goofy hero can provide a counterbalance, preventing the narrative from becoming overly heavy. However, if the story's overall tone is too serious or emotional, the hero's humor might seem out of place and disrupt the intended mood.

Disrespectful: Ensure his humor isn't hurtful or disrespectful to others. His jokes should uplift and entertain, rather than belittle or demean. In the case when the Slacker takes his joke too far, it should be an opportunity for growth, and he should likely have to face the consequences of his hurtful words or actions, especially when it impacts relationships.

Heroine who is too uptight: If the goofy hero's personality clashes with that of a love interest who simply never loosens up, the romantic chemistry may end up lacking. Any contrast of personality can create opportunities for humor, tension, and change in the characters, but if the love interest never learns to appreciate the hero for his less-than-serious side, it makes the longevity of the relationship incredibly difficult to buy into.

Contrived situations: If the Slacker's goofiness is used solely for comedic effect without a natural context, it might feel contrived and detract from the story's authenticity. In addition, if his goofiness is portrayed as excessive or unrealistic, it might come across as forced or irritating to some readers.

COMMONLY PAIRED TROPES

The Slacker pairs well with a lot of the same tropes as other Bad Boys, and it may even be combined with other Bad Boy tropes such as the Playboy.

Because the Slacker typically needs to find the value in applying himself and reaching his true potential, he is often paired with a heroine that will bring it out of him. Any trope that would highlight Opposites Attract such as the Bookworm/Nerd/Geek (or any other Passion and Competence trope) or the Girl Next Door will be successful in creating that dynamic. When the contrast between these personalities creates a clash and makes sparks fly, it may lead to an Enemies to Lovers situation.

As a note, the Slacker generally doesn't stack with Passion and Competence tropes, because of the intense nature of these careers and the reader expectations that accompany them. After all, the primary draw of these tropes is to demonstrate the competence and passion of the trope character . . . not exactly compatible with the Slacker.

POTENTIAL WOUNDS

Cracking under pressure
Poor judgment leading to unintended consequences
Growing up in the shadow of a successful sibling
Declaring bankruptcy
Failing at school or work
Public humiliation

COMMON TRAITS

Apathetic	Humorous	Relaxed
Cool	Indifferent	Easygoing
Laid back	Lazy	Unconcerned
Carefree	Unmotivated	Irresponsible
Nonchalant	Casual	Effortless

CINNAMON ROLL

THIS TROPE FULFILLS THE READER'S DESIRE TO FIND COMPANIONSHIP, KINDNESS, AND SUPPORT FROM THEIR PARTNER

A Cinnamon Roll hero is a character type that is a relatively recent designation in the romance genre. A Cinnamon Roll is characterized by his sweetness, kindness, and overall wholesome nature. As the term cinnamon roll implies, these heroes are soft-hearted, caring, and genuinely good, much like the comforting and warm qualities associated with the pastry. Sometimes, these characters are written with burnt or crusty edges, but once you are on the inside, they are all sweet and soft.

Cinnamon Rolls are often supportive, considerate, and emotionally available. They tend to prioritize the well-being and happiness of their romantic interest, often going out of their way to help them or even just listen. In contrast to the brooding bad boy, the cinnamon roll hero tends to focus on building healthy and nurturing relationships. Don't underestimate his willingness or ability to defend the honor of his lady—he'll just do it in the most honorable way he knows how.

This might also be considered something of a Boy Next Door type. These are the guys you want in your friend group, who every grandma is trying to set you up with, and who you automatically assume is great with kids.

WHY READERS LOVE IT

In a world where negativity can be prevalent, readers appreciate characters who embody positivity, kindness, and compassion. In contrast to more complex or morally ambiguous characters, the appeal of the cinnamon roll hero lies in his purity, sincerity, and ability to provide a sense of comfort and safety in the story. They have a natural balance between their strength and vulnerability. They are capable of being protective and assertive when needed, yet they also show a compassionate and emotionally available side that makes them highly relatable and likable to readers.

Readers are drawn to these characters because they represent a type of love that is gentle, understanding, and unwavering. A cinnamon roll hero is characterized by a set of endearing traits that make him wholesome, kind-hearted, and emotionally supportive. He is the heroine's biggest supporter and is especially thoughtful and generous. These heroes tend to be gentle in their actions and interactions. Readers appreciate their ability to handle delicate situations with care and without resorting to aggression or hostility.

READER EXPECTATIONS

While Cinnamon Roll heroes will nearly always start out as kind and loving humans from the outset of your romance novel, readers will still expect to see some element of personal growth, often involving overcoming personal challenges and becoming even more confident in their own skin.

These heroes are often part of healthy and supportive relationships. Readers anticipate seeing both partners uplift and encourage each other, contributing to a positive and mutually beneficial dynamic. When conflicts arise, readers expect cinnamon roll heroes to approach the situation with maturity and a desire to resolve issues peacefully. They typically avoid unnecessary drama and instead focus on communication and understanding.

Cinnamon Roll heroes are known for their unwavering kindness and ability to empathize with others. Readers expect them to treat not only the romantic interest but also other characters with respect and consideration. The stories featuring Cinnamon Roll heroes tend to have an uplifting and heartwarming quality that resonates with readers seeking a feel-good experience.

These heroes typically have a strong sense of right and wrong. They make decisions based on their moral compass, which resonates with readers who admire characters with ethical principles.

If uncovering the vulnerability of Bad Boys is like peeling back the layers of an onion, then Cinnamon Rolls are wearing their hearts on their sleeve. These men don't necessarily play hard to get, and they don't play games or manipulate the love interest. They aren't afraid to show their vulnerability to the love interest and share their feelings, and it's this emotional openness that creates a deeper connection between the character and the readers.

COMMON PITFALLS

Sensitive in the wrong situations: Just because your Cinnamon roll is genuine and kind doesn't mean he is having emotionally charged conversations while hanging out in the locker room. He's still a guy and unless the time is right, he's keeping his emotions close to the vest. It's often only the love interest who will see the center of the Cinnamon Roll—which is, of course, the very best part.

Lack of complexity: The easygoing nature of these heroes sometimes leaves authors with less angst and conflict for a significant character arc. Just remember that easygoing does not mean shallow and predictable. In fact, sometimes what's happening on the facade can be the complete opposite to the interior struggle. It is important to find ways that these characters can surprise your heroine and the reader.

Lack of realism/relatability: Because these characters are very level-headed and good to the core, some readers find them unrealistic or have difficulty relating them. Just remember that there can be a lot of complexity behind someone's actions. By revealing backstory, motivations, and wounds, you can give your reader a much fuller picture of who your hero is and why it is that he is so darned good all the time.

Not to mention, this may be one of the very issues your heroine finds with him! It's not uncommon for people to be suspect of an overly kind or selfless person; it's your job as the author to prove that your cinnamon roll is truly genuine.

Lack of conflict: When writing a Cinnamon Roll, it can be difficult to create compelling enough conflict to sustain the entire novel. In most romances using this trope, the conflict will be driven by external forces or focused on the internal struggle of the heroine. Though, you will find plenty of Cinnamon Roll heroes who resent their mild nature and struggle to accept their own goodness as a strength and not a weakness.

COMMONLY PAIRED TROPES

One of the most popular appearances of the Cinnamon Roll trope is having it paired with the Alpha Male, (aka an Alpha Roll). These characters are tough, confident, and unrelenting—except when it comes to their love interest or family. This is a cinnamon roll character with burnt edges, so to speak.

The Cinnamon Roll also pairs nicely with any sort of "good guy" tropes where you want to see the genuine kindness shine through. Tropes like Friends to More, Single Parent, or Counselor/Pastor would fit here.

Additionally, trope pairings where the Cinnamon Roll aspect of the character is an unexpected dimension of another character trope are popular, such as a Cinnamon Roll Celebrity or a Cinnamon Roll Billionaire.

POTENTIAL WOUNDS

Getting dumped
Infidelity
Unrequited love
Misplaced loyalty
Becoming a caregiver at an early age
Missing a major life opportunity because of indecision or passivity
A parent's divorce

COMMON TRAITS

Honorable	Selfless	Sweet
Humble	Ethical	Considerate
Unassuming	Vulnerable	Altruistic
Kind	Compassionate	Modest
Gentle	Empathetic	Supportive

DAMSEL IN DISTRESS

THIS TROPE FULFILLS THE READER'S DESIRE FOR A DEPENDABLE HERO WHO OFFERS COMFORT, PROVISION, AND SAFETY

The Damsel in Distress has existed as an archetype in literature and media for centuries, often found in romantic and adventure stories. It refers to a female character who finds herself in a situation of vulnerability or impending danger, requiring rescue or protection by a hero. In many ways, this character trope has evolved from its original portrayal of an archetype woman who is helpless, passive, and in need of external intervention to overcome her challenges. Today's Damsels may be facing extreme danger or other circumstances beyond their control, but that does not mean that they won't put up a fight, whether it's physically or intellectually.

The Damsel is often treated as if her only virtue is beauty, and it is your job as the author to reveal her as so much more. Subverting or reimagining the trope in fresh ways can provide a modern twist that resonates with a wider range of readers.

WHY READERS LOVE IT

As one of the longest known tropes in literature, the Damsel in Distress offers a bit of nostalgia for those who love classic stories of brave and heroic knights fighting off dragons and evil lords to save their lady. This trope easily satisfies one of the original appeals of romance novels—the yearning for a strong male who will challenge the heroine on her own terms, but is also virile, protective, and able to rescue her from distress.

Almost as the opposite perspective of the bodyguard trope, this trope also stirs the emotions of readers who swoon over protective, nurturing men and send their hearts all aflutter when the hero finally sweeps the princess into his arms to carry her to safety—not to mention the sacrifices and obstacles he must face on the journey to her rescue.

The source of distress for these leading ladies tends to be captivity or some immediate peril. Because of this element, readers who love adventure and epic heroes will appreciate the draw of these novels when done well. For this reason, Damsel in Distress stories should include moments of suspense, drama, and danger that will keep readers engaged.

READER EXPECTATIONS

As much as the Damsel in a harrowing situation is crucial to this trope, so is the dashing and brave hero. Whether your Damsel sits around waiting for her rescue or actively works to secure her own freedom, she must get her rescue scene with the hero. Now . . . if you really wanted to shake things up . . . you could always flip the roles and have your strong-willed heroine rescue the Dude in Distress. In either case, their separation must culminate in a moment of rescue and reunification.

These heroines may sometimes come across as more passive, but when done well, their passivity is only a front for everything bubbling to the surface at the moment of greatest impact. In fact, it is more common for these heroines to possess a ton of spunk and a stubborn streak that comes out as defiance and an unwillingness to lay down and be captured . . . nonetheless, their efforts will be overcome by their captors. In this way, despite her willingness and efforts to fight her way out her plight, there is an inherent helplessness and lack of control over her physical circumstance. Being unable to escape her predicament does not make these heroines weak, but rather it means that they must learn to accept some outside help.

As this trope has evolved, it has become increasingly important to find a balance between the Damsel's reliance on the rescue of others and the ability to use her own abilities. Readers are unlikely to get behind a character who takes but never gives back. This may extend to the romantic relationship, with the hero and heroine sharing some level of respect, support and trust in one another.

COMMON PITFALLS

Too traditional: Just as some readers love these stories for their classic appeal, others consider those same elements to be antiquated and detrimental to the promotion of more progressive gender roles.

Lack of agency: Even among fans of the trope, authors may draw ire for weak heroines, lacking in agency, growth, or wit. Readers find it difficult to buy into a character who seems to be entirely at the mercy of her circumstances and the rescue of a dashing hero.

Limited character development: Because of the stereotypes of the Damsel in Distress and the fact that these stories tend to contain quite a bit of adventure/external plot, the character development of the heroine may get lost in the mix.

Functional prop: Sometimes the heroine can appear to function more as a motivation for the hero's journey of transformation rather than a fully fleshed out character in her own right.

COMMONLY PAIRED TROPES

Since the Damsel in Distress character is naturally designed to fit a character that is protective and fierce, it is commonly found alongside *Tough Guy* tropes (Pirate, Viking, Highlander, Bodyguard), or other tropes with physically strong heroes—Men in Uniform, Woodsman/Lumberjack, and Alpha Male to name a few.

You are also likely to see this in historical settings such as Medieval, Regency, or Western, and it is a commonly used archetype in fairy tales, making it inherent in certain Fairy Tale Retellings.

POTENTIAL WOUNDS

Domestic abuse
Being stalked/victimized
Experiencing poverty
A toxic relationship
Abandonment due to pregnancy
Financial ruin due to spouse's irresponsibility
Having one's ideas or work stolen

COMMON TRAITS

Vulnerable	Resilient	Submissive
Innocent	Gentle	Fearful
Timid	Graceful	Trusting
Helpless	Caring	Naïve
Sensitive	Compassionate	Delicate

ECCENTRIC

THIS TROPE FEEDS INTO THE READER'S DESIRE TO BE LOVED FOR WHO THEY TRULY ARE

The Eccentric is a character who is known primarily for their unique and typically unconventional perspective or behavior. They deeply value their individuality and usually consider their quirks as a strength rather than an oddity. The character's eccentricity may be prominent in their worldview, interactions, hobbies, interests, appearance, or style.

This character trope adds a layer of intrigue, humor, and distinctiveness to the narrative, making the story and characters more engaging for readers. They might exhibit social awkwardness or have difficulty conforming to societal norms, leading to charming or humorous interactions. Beneath their eccentricities, these characters often have deeper emotions and vulnerabilities that are revealed as the romance develops.

These characters may have some overlap with the Nerd/Genius/Bookworm character trope.

WHY READERS LOVE IT

Readers who value creativity are often drawn to these characters, as they are likely to find unexpected and ingenious solutions for both everyday and major problems.

The authenticity of these characters makes them incredibly endearing to the reader and love interest alike. These characters often encourage growth, open-mindedness, and the exploration of unique connections, making the romance novel more captivating and enjoyable for readers.

In addition to providing humor and comedic relief, the complexity of the Eccentric often challenges the love interest or other supporting characters to reconsider preconceived notions and perspectives.

READER EXPECTATIONS

Something about the Eccentric should set them apart from the other characters, and even real people. It could be their style of dress, their behavior, or even their priorities. This requires understanding and communicating to readers what constitutes as normal in your story world—and this may vary greatly depending on setting. Things that may seem totally outside the norm in a Regency romance—such as a heroine who chooses independence and personal ambition over marriage—would be far less unconventional in a contemporary romance.

Readers expect a combination of uniqueness, emotional depth, and growth that embraces and celebrates the Eccentric's quirks and authenticity. They want to know how the love interest is affected by the trope character's behavior, whether it's fascination, shock, confusion, or acceptance.

The oddities that mark these characters' personalities will likely be rooted in something that occurred in their past. Readers want to know how this quirky personality has set them apart, how it developed, or how it has affected the character.

It is expected that many or most of the interactions this character has with other characters will be unconventional, resulting in moments of humor, surprise, and even vulnerability.

COMMON PITFALLS

Comedic prop: While most readers appreciate the lighthearted nature of the Eccentric character, authors should be cautious of veering into slapstick or outrageous territory. This often makes the character seem more like a prop than a functional human being.

Destination Crazy Town: While your character may seem outlandish and unlike anyone the reader has ever met, understand that *eccentric* does not mean *crazy*. Even if your character is perceived as crazy, make sure that you give them some strengths to be demonstrated as virtues, solidifying their lucidity and (at least some degree of) soundness of mind.

Manic pixie dream girl: This iteration of the Eccentric trope was widely used in the early 2000s, and it has since become a major pet peeve of readers. The Manic Pixie Dream Girl is not only quirky, but she is stunningly beautiful, energetic (almost childlike), and generally cheerful. Pairing the Eccentric with the broody, isolated or cynical hero often results in manic-pixie-dream-girl vibes; but the more well-developed your character is, the less likely you are to fall into this trap of a woman who functions primarily to add excitement, and therefore meaning, to the hero's dull life.

COMMONLY PAIRED TROPES

While there are certainly examples of two eccentric individuals finding love (such as Juno MacGuff and Paulie Bleeker in *Juno*), this trope is often paired with Opposites Attract tropes like

ECCENTRIC

Grumpy/Sunshine. The love interest's stability and the Eccentric's spontaneity lead to some clashing, but ultimately they will help each other grow and become more grounded.

Placing an eccentric character in a new environment or situation where their quirks stand out even more is commonly done using the Fish Out of Water trope, and it typically leads to comedic and endearing moments. Because of the Eccentric's habit of operating outside of societal norms, this trope lends itself well to the Bad Boy/Rebel trope. Both tropes can explore themes such as authenticity, defying conventions, and self-acceptance.

The Eccentric may also be paired with certain *Passion and Competence* character tropes, especially the Nerd/Genius/Bookworm character. Their unconventional way of thinking accentuates their quirks, but it also proves to be a strength in coming up with unique solutions. Pair this with exceptional intelligence and competence, and you'll have a truly captivating hero or heroine.

POTENTIAL WOUNDS

Growing up in the public eye
A nomadic childhood
Social difficulties
Being bullied
Being rejected by one's peers
A learning disability

COMMON TRAITS

Unique	Routine	Flighty
Confident	Memorable	Unpredictable
Opinionated	Offbeat	Spontaneous
Fond of rituals	Quirky	Creative
	Genuine	Unconventional

THE GRUMP

THIS TROPE FULFILLS THE READER'S DESIRE TO INITIMATELY KNOW SOMEONE THAT KEEPS MOST PEOPLE AT A DISTANCE

In the most basic terms, the Grump is a glass-half-empty kind of guy (or gal). This character doesn't typically make a great first impression. He may be a neighbor, coworker, or boss, or he may be a part of the same social or professional circles as the love interest. The point is, no matter how unappealing building a rapport with the Grump seems, your characters will be somewhat thrown together by their circumstances and forced to interact.

WHY READERS LOVE IT

Not all romance stories featuring the Grump will have a Grumpy/Sunshine dynamic, but regardless of the love interest's personality type, there should be some balance achieved by pairing them together. Readers delight in a romance that makes both parties stronger.

One of the most surprising and endearing traits of the Grump is their hidden capacity for charm and kindness. It's a revelation that slowly unfolds as the layers of skepticism peel away. As your characters find themselves drawn into the gravitational field of the Grump's world, they start glimpsing the cracks in the armor—moments where a genuine smile sneaks onto their lips or a rare chuckle escapes from their throat. Perhaps they secretly donate to a local charity but would rather chew glass than admit it. It's these little paradoxes that draw people in, allowing them to see beyond the surly exterior and recognize the complex, multi-faceted individual lurking beneath.

Readers love to see the Grump in an unexpectedly sweet or thoughtful moment. Doing something that shows respect, care, tenderness (or any other admirable and swoon-worthy quality) throws other characters off and endears the reader to the Grump, all while livening up the narrative. When readers and characters are expecting a harsh response and they are met instead with a soft touch, they are primed for the moment that will eventually melt your grump's hardened heart.

Double up on the reader's buy-in with these unexpectedly sweet moment by keeping it from the love interest. Just a flicker of softness shown through internal dialogue or ambiguous body language can reveal to the reader that there's a lot more going on under the surface, even if the Grump isn't quite ready to reveal this softer side to anyone else. The grump nearly always brushes off the appreciation or recognition of those thoughtful gestures, sometimes even regretting that he let himself show he cared. All of which makes the heroine (and the reader) desperate to understand why he is so gruff.

READER EXPECTATIONS

The Grump will almost certainly make a poor first impression on the love interest, but he can't make such a poor impression on the reader that they fail to root for him. Be sure to include an interaction early in the book that demonstrates the Grump's soft side, even if very few people ever experience this aspect of his personality. It could be a family member, close friend, or someone in a vulnerable situation. Show that the character does indeed care and consider others, even if their outward demeanor doesn't match.

Readers want to understand *why* your character is so negative all the time—if they can't empathize or understand his outlook and behavior, the negativity simply becomes stifling and exhausting. This reason may be implied or it may be outright stated, but before we can understand why the love interest should give your character a chance, readers need to understand why *they* should give him a chance.

Give your grump a flaw to overcome, something to fix, and some goal that the reader can root for them to achieve. Setting your character up to be the underdog, handing them some injustice to overcome (even if it's just never getting through the coffee line in the breakroom before the brew turns cold), and simply making them charming and entertaining are all effective ways to make sure your reader cares about your character and wants them to succeed in all their grumpy glory.

As your character begins to thaw out under the loving tenderness of the love interest, they should begin to experience a change in perspective. It's not just that the Grump's circumstances change, it's that he experiences a true change of heart.

BREAKDOWN OF ARCHETYPES

Abrasive grump—At first glance, the Abrasive Grump seems to carry an ever-present cloud of discontent around them like a protective shield. Their demeanor is a masterclass in cynicism, each interaction tainted by a biting sarcasm that could strip paint off walls. They navigate the world armed with a repertoire of eye rolls, heavy sighs, and a knack for retorts that could send even the most confident soul into a bewildered silence. The Abrasive Grump's comments often cut through pretense and social niceties, leaving a wake of uncomfortable truths in their path. This abrasiveness might be directed at everyone around them, stemming from a general mistrust of human intentions, or it could be a defense mechanism developed over years of disappointments. Yet, beneath that thorny exterior, there's a complexity to the Grump that makes them intriguing. A life marked by experiences that have made them so abrasive has also given them a unique perspective, a resilience forged in the fires of adversity.

Lovable grump—While the outer layer might appear weathered by life's annoyances, those fortunate enough to be let in will discover a steadfast friend whose loyalty and protectiveness are unmatched. The Grump's world might be peppered with minor complaints and amusingly grumbly comments, giving them a reputation as someone who's quick to find fault. Yet, paradoxically, the very same people who receive these grumbles often find themselves wrapped in a comforting cocoon of care. The Grump is the one who secretly checks in on a friend when they're sick, offering a hearty bowl of homemade soup with a side of gentle teasing.

Those who've managed to breach the Grump's carefully constructed walls and see the person behind the gruff exterior are adamant defenders of his character and goodness. This type of Grump might wish they could be grumpier, believing that their hardened exterior could shield them from further emotional entanglements. But try as they might, the goodness within them refuses to be stifled. And it's this inner kindness that draws people in, creating an unbreakable bond.

Guarded grump—The Guarded Grump's heart is wrapped in layers of barbed wire, a fortress built from past disappointments and betrayals. Trust is not easily earned in their world, and anyone attempting to penetrate their defenses must navigate a treacherous emotional maze. The Grump might have been hurt before—perhaps they've experienced loss, heartbreak, or a series of letdowns that have led them to adopt this guarded approach. They've honed the skill of reading people's intentions, detecting ulterior motives with a surgeon's precision. While their guarded nature might seem like a challenge, it's also a testament to their self-preservation instincts. And as your characters gradually earn the Grump's trust, they'll discover a vulnerability that's both tender and beautiful. The moments when the Grump lets their guard down become pivotal turning points, painting a picture of a soul craving connection but fearful of the scars that can come with it.

COMMON PITFALLS

He's mean, but he's wounded: Sympathy alone isn't enough to make readers care about the Grump. Give him a worthy goal, strong motivations, or even a sense of humor or manners. Show the reader someone who *does* like the character (and make sure it's someone we can respect the opinion of), and you'll immediately tip the reader off to the fact that there's something worth finding under the surface of these Negative Nellies.

A bridge too far: Be careful not to make your hero do anything that makes him *too unlikeable.* You don't want to anger readers or turn them off to the character, and in turn, the romance.

Abusive cycle: Your hero will likely botch a few (or several) attempts at winning over the heroine once he decides he's all in. But be sure that it doesn't become a constant cycle of him acting like a jerk and asking forgiveness without ever changing. This can quickly turn readers off, make them question the heroine's judgment and can even come off as somewhat abusive. If you feel it is truly necessary for your character to do something that may genuinely anger readers, consider having it happen off the page and telling the reader about it afterward. This little bit of distance can make the reaction of the reader less visceral, and the severity of the crime feel slightly more forgivable.

Excessively rude, broody, or abrasive: This trope is not an excuse for bad behavior and selfishness—if your grump acts this way, there should be some form of consequence/atonement. Balance these less inviting interactions with moments of warmth, humor and vulnerability with a supporting character to show the love interest that there is some potential for true connection. Sometimes it seems that even the reader never learns to like the Grump, let alone love him—and if she doesn't like him, why should readers? As the narrative progresses, your grump should grow decidedly less grumpy, and the attraction and emotional connection should grow deeper.

COMMONLY PAIRED TROPES

The most obvious hallmark of the Grump can be seen in its pairing with the Grumpy/Sunshine trope. In this relational trope, the negativity or cynicism of the Grump is paired with a character who radiates positivity, optimism and . . . well, sunshine. This may be played off as something of an Enemies to Lovers situation, or the characters may just simply not hit it off upon first meeting. In either case, the dynamic results in the love interests learning to balance one another.

It can also be paired with just about any setting trope, but combinations with Small-Town, Workplace, Ranch and Christmas are especially popular. It is also used often with the Lone Wolf trope and *Emotional Baggage* tropes, such as the Widow(er), Single Parent, and Seasoned Characters.

Tropes that force interaction with the Grump such as Workplace, Boss/Employee, Caregiver/Nanny, or Neighbors are well-paired and create plenty of opportunity for your grump to soften toward the love interest, and vice versa. Situational tropes like Forced Proximity, Matchmaker, and Marriage of Convenience may also be used to the same effect.

POTENTIAL WOUNDS:

Making a very public mistake
Being falsely accused of a crime
Being let down by a trusted organization or social system
Misplaced loyalty/betrayal

COMMON TRAITS

Aloof	Protective	Unyielding
Guarded	Contradictory	Prickly
Cynical	Resistant	Loyal
Jaded	Stubborn	
Blunt	Endearing	
Abrasive	Complex	

LONE WOLF/RECLUSE

---

*THIS TROPE FEEDS INTO THE
READER'S DESIRE FOR A
RELATIONSHIP THAT IS INTIMATE
AND EXCLUSIVE*

The Lone Wolf may be an actual recluse or simply emotionally closed off. In either case, this hero (or heroine) has physical barriers, emotional barriers, or both, shutting out the world and its influence. They are unwilling or feel unable to engage with society. These characters can be further broken down into two categories: the Forced Recluse, and the Preferred Recluse.

The Forced Recluse does not choose to be alone but has been shunned or rejected by society. The Preferred Recluse simply chooses solitude.

Both may be the result of a past hurt or sin, but it may also be due to extreme introversion or shyness, eccentricity, pride, obsessive focus on their work, or simply placing privacy above all other priorities.

The nature of isolation means that these characters often become regimented and stuck in their ways, not only hesitant to let others in, but also hesitant to change. As the name suggests, these heroes prefer to work alone and are usually slow to trust others. They are accustomed to doing everything themselves and will not respond well to an offer of help or a feisty heroine/pushy hero inserting themselves into their problems. Despite their difficulty in connecting with others, they tend to be impressive and dominating characters who will draw readers in with their self-sufficiency and surprising confidence.

WHY READERS LOVE IT

The solitary and enigmatic nature of the Lone Wolf engages readers' curiosity and draws them into the character. As their motivations, hidden depths, and old wounds are uncovered, readers are pulled in by the potential for redemption and healing.

These heroes may be lonely, but even in their solitude, their strength of character shines through. Readers love to see these characters overcome challenges and adversity, so be sure to include moments that highlight these admirable traits in your Lone Wolf.

Given the often troubled past of these heroes, readers easily become invested in their potential for redemption and the healing power of love. Allow readers a full glimpse of how your character's past has shaped their reclusiveness so that they can form a deep emotional connection.

Readers love to watch the hero on their journey from solitude to opening up to love and emotional vulnerability as they learn to let someone (the love interest) into their life. The love interest's challenge of breaking down the hero's emotional barriers and reaching his heart gives the reader something to root for. Not to mention, once the Lone Wolf lets someone in, they tend to be fiercely loyal. And who doesn't love a loyal hero? *Swoon.* When it comes down to it, the very act of the Lone Wolf sacrificing their need or desire for solitude for the sake of love highlights the depth of their commitment.

READER EXPECTATIONS

This character's arc often involves a thawing or softening toward the love interest (and others in general), as they must work to overcome their isolationist habits and lifestyle in order to let someone else into their life and trust them with their heart. This is not an easy process, though, and you can expect to see them retreating back into their guarded ways before fully letting anyone in. Because the process of learning to value the support of others and learning to rely on community will take time, this is often paired with a slow burn romance.

You will want to really flesh out the emotional wound and backstory of these characters, as it will contribute greatly to their loner habits and their methods for guarding themselves against human connection. This wound will also be at the center of the divide between your love interests, and it will lead to highly emotional and pivotal scenes.

These characters are often so defined by their pain (after all, they have completely changed their life in order to cope with it), that they are faced with an existential crisis at the thought of overcoming it. In other words, the Lone Wolf has rooted their identity in their emotional wound. Because of this, you will not see the Lone Wolf reaching out, even when they do encounter someone willing to engage with them, and it will take much pursuit on the part of the love interest to draw the Lone Wolf out. It is the romantic relationship, perhaps in conjunction with a new friendship or community, that will make your lone wolf realize the need to overcome their reason for isolation. This realization often comes when their friendship or love interest is put in a perilous situation— when the people they have (reluctantly) grown to care for are put in harm's way, they are suddenly willing to admit that they need that connection to others. This allows them to overcome the pain that they have identified with for so long in order to save the love they never thought they wanted.

COMMON PITFALLS

He just hasn't found the* right *person: Don't try to rely on a simple "I don't like people" explanation. Man wasn't created to be alone, and we don't end up that way without some serious hurts . . . your character will be infinitely more interesting when you have nuances and a backstory to dig into in order to overcome their isolation. Telling the story of a man who only ever learned to appreciate one person—the woman of his dreams—is not only completely unrealistic, it's boring.

Suddenly social: Your lone wolf will be resistant to the pursuit of others to draw him/her into community and relationship. Although it will take time for them to break old habits, don't allow them to repeat the same pattern over and over—any self-respecting person will eventually give up when met with the same unsuccessful result at every attempt. So be sure that with each interaction, there is some change in your character and some point of growth—even if they remain reluctant to reveal their slowly changing heart. In other words, while your character will not immediately be open to relationships, they should begin to adapt to interacting with others and they learn to "lone wolf" in ways that allow them to engage in their circumstances without a complete and total retreat.

It's Me. I'm the problem: In literary fiction, tv shows, movies and other genres such as thriller or mystery, the Lone Wolf archetype is often made to be an antihero. While this does make for a complex and engaging protagonist, it is difficult to pull this off in a romance novel. You may have more success with this strategy in cross-genre romance, but due to the need for your reader to connect with and root for your protagonists to find love with one another, it is incredibly challenging to successfully write a hero who your reader can hate and still hope for his romantic success.

Excessively rude, broody or abrasive: This trope is not an excuse for bad behavior and selfishness—if your lone wolf acts this way, there should be some form of consequence/atonement. While your lone wolf will naturally seem somewhat unapproachable, he shouldn't be unlikeable. Balance these less inviting interactions with moments of warmth, humor, and vulnerability with a supporting character to show the love interest that there is some potential for true connection.

COMMONLY PAIRED TROPES

The Lone Wolf is a popular internal character trope that pairs well in most situations. It is especially common with Cowboys and in Western settings and other tropes with strong heroes like Bodyguard and Lumberjack.

Many of the *Money, Money* tropes lend themselves to a Lone Wolf trope, especially Billionaire or Musician.

Often, because their reclusive nature is due to a deep emotional wound, Lone Wolf is often paired with a Widow(er) trope.

Because the Lone Wolf often needs a catalyst for coming out of their self-imposed exile, tropes that bring the love interest crashing into their orbit work well. Amnesia or Runaway Bride would be good examples of this.

POTENTIAL WOUNDS:

Accidentally killing someone/failing to save someone
Cracking under pressure
Making a very public mistake
Growing up in the public eye
Being falsely accused of a crime
Being let down by a trusted organization or social system
Misplaced loyalty/betrayal

COMMON TRAITS

Aloof	Unconventional	Resourceful
Guarded	Determined	Self reliant
Cynical	Disciplined	Enigmatic
Jaded	Intimidating	Private
Blunt	Abrasive	Upright

RAGS TO RICHES/LOST HEIR(ESS)

THIS TROPE FEEDS INTO THE READER'S DESIRE FOR A BRIGHT FUTURE TO EMERGE FROM ANY CIRCUMSTANCE

These two tropes follow a similar character arc, as the hero or heroine must adapt to new circumstances that are at sharp contrast from the life they've previously known.

A lost heir or heiress story is almost always one in which the main character discovers their true identity as heir to a grand fortune. In a Rags to Riches story, it may be the result of a lifetime of hard work on the part of your main character, a matter of chance, charity, or something else that happens upon them.

In any case, these tropes introduce a seemingly ordinary character who finds their world turned upside down by extraordinary circumstances. These characters come from humble beginnings, and they should have relatable goals, dreams, and struggles that readers can connect with. Introduce the protagonist in their initial state of poverty or modest circumstances, and use these opening scenes to show their determination and resilience despite hardships.

WHY READERS LOVE IT

Readers love that these stories are heartwarming, and above all, hopeful. The reinforced, hard-fought love between hero and heroine leaves the reader with a sense of fulfillment and the belief that their love will endure despite any challenges or circumstance. The contrast between their initial struggles and eventual triumphs creates a compelling narrative arc that captures readers' hearts and imagination.

These characters are no strangers to adversity, and they often have a very underdog appeal to them, endearing them to readers and making their happily ever after oh, so satisfying.

The reunification theme of the Lost Heir trope is especially popular with readers, who love to see families reunited, characters connect with their true heritage, and reach untapped potential.

Mystery and suspense lovers may also gravitate toward the intrigue and hidden identity elements of these stories. Often, these characters must uncover a puzzle of their lineage and face the challenge of discovering that they are not the person they knew themselves to be.

READER EXPECTATIONS

There is typically a heavy emphasis on personal growth and transformation while remaining grounded in the qualities that made them who they are—or, if they were awful before, understanding that changed circumstances don't change the heart, and they must find it within themself to be the person they aspire to be. By the end of the story, they should undergo a series of transformations mentally, morally/spiritually, and obviously physically.

You should portray the protagonist's journey from rags to riches in a gradual and believable way. Highlight their reactions to newfound wealth, whether it's awe, disbelief, or discomfort. Showcase how their world changes and how they adapt. These changes should inevitably create a stark contrast with the love interest, whether they are watching someone they have already known and loved change into someone they hardly recognize or learning that their privileged way of life is something that someone might actually struggle to embrace. The contrast may be between the difference in background or the difference in current circumstances, and it should create tension as well as some degree of fascination.

Be sure to explore this internal struggle as they navigate their new life, interactions, and relationships. Dig deep into insecurities, doubts, and fears about fitting in, as well as concerns about losing their true self. As you introduce obstacles and challenges, they should put the development of the romance and the character's search for identity/personal growth at odds. The trope character will likely struggle for most of the book to make decisions between their core values/known principles and new societal expectation. In the end, they should preserve authenticity while embracing the positive changes and learning to navigate and cope with new challenges. The couple must be able to learn from one another and find common ground in order to succeed in their relationship.

COMMON PITFALLS

Too convenient: Sometimes the circumstances of the protagonist's rise to fortune feels too convenient, unbelievable, or contrived. Be sure to think out a plausible reason for the character's change of fortune, or else highlight the oddity of it.

Lack of personal growth: Focusing too heavily on the external transformation (in appearance, culture, or lifestyle) can lead to underdeveloped characters when using these tropes. Readers need to connect with the hero or heroine on a deeper level to feel invested in their journey and happily ever after.

Shallow motivations: The reasons behind the character's desire for wealth or success should be well-explored. If their motivations are shallow or one-dimensional, it can weaken the emotional resonance of the story. These stories have the potential to explore deep themes like identity, socioeconomic dynamic, and the meaning of success and happiness. Failing to develop these themes may also lead to a narrative that feels too shallow for readers to connect with.

Lack of conflict: The whirlwind nature of these stories sometimes makes it seem as if all the troubles in the world melt away for these characters when their fortune changes. If the rise to riches or royalty doesn't lead to meaningful challenges, it will result in a lackluster narrative.

COMMONLY PAIRED TROPES

The Lost Heir(ess) trope is especially common in Historical or Royalty romance, where bloodline trumped everything. However it is also commonly paired with other *Money, Money* tropes, if we meet the protagonist shortly after or before their windfall, such as sudden Celebrity status or a casual investor who just hit it big on the stock market to become a Billionaire.

The Rags to Riches character is often paired with tropes that force them to reconcile their past with their suddenly different-than-expected future such as Coming Home, Fish Out of Water, or All Grown Up.

This trope is also commonly paired with Second Chance romance, with the character forced to come to the realization that their money or status (or lack thereof) does not define them.

POTENTIAL WOUNDS:

Declaring bankruptcy
Living in poverty

Being adopted
Being abandoned or rejected by a parent
Being forced to leave one's homeland
Being sent away as a child

COMMON TRAITS

Optimistic	Adaptable	Courageous
Humble	Authentic	Empathetic
Resilient	Determined	Spirited
Positive	Tenacious	Open minded
Hopeful	Resourceful	Hardworking

CHAPTER 12

MEN (AND WOMEN) IN UNIFORM

---

*THESE TROPES FEED THE READER'S
DESIRE TO BE SAVED AND
PROTECTED*

The Men (and Women) in Uniform character trope encompasses a diverse range of characters and occupations. From the informant falling in love with the officer assigned to protect her to the naval officer candidate finding inspiration and love in a townie, the possibilities for storytelling are endless. A character's chosen career can serve as a source of strength or vulnerability, shaping their personality and contributing to their character arc.

A person's occupation and the environment they navigate daily affects their thoughts, actions, and reactions to the world. In the case of Men (and women) in Uniform, the occupation becomes the defining trope, intricately woven into every aspect of the character's identity and role in the story.

Within this character trope, the occupations themselves serve as tropes, divided into three primary categories: Military, Law Enforcement, and Firefighters/EMTs. While some elements may overlap between each category, there are distinctive qualities that make each one unique. We'll first evaluate the group as a whole, then isolate and celebrate the distinct traits of each category.

WHY READERS LOVE IT

We love a good hero. And we mean a *heroic* hero. A main character who is brave and selfless, putting themself in harm's way for the greater good. Whether it is running into burning buildings, literally hunting the bad guys, or simply protecting someone vulnerable— we admire them.

These heroes are engaging and multi-dimensional, and in the case of the male main character—they make the reader feel protected and safe. These heroes command respect, and we love them for it.

What else draws readers to this genre though? One common piece of these tropes that is often overlooked, but beloved by readers, is the "brotherhood" relationships formed by characters within these organizations. One way you can make your Military, Law Enforcement, or Firefighter romances grab the reader more fully is to really show the bond between your main character and the minor characters they are serving alongside. These characters are putting their lives on the line with each other, and it is a great way to show attributes about your character in an authentic and enjoyable way.

READER EXPECTATIONS

When readers pick up a book featuring a main character who is in uniform, the expectation is that their profession has an impact on the story, or at the very least on the character themselves.

If your firefighter is a Firefighter in name only, but we never see him in the line of duty or hanging out at the fire station, then there may be a sense of disappointment from the reader that you didn't deliver on the promise of a Firefighter main character.

The same goes for a Military hero. If his military service is not obvious from his actions, thoughts, or how he spends his time, then what did it matter if he was a former Air Force lieutenant? If you are promising the reader a Man (or Woman) in Uniform, be sure to deliver it.

The nature of these professions all require the hero/heroine to overcome obstacles to their relationships and they may face a variety of difficulties to keep the relationship strong. Their career is likely a result or a cause of their wound and motivations.

Your character can have any personality, interests, or belief system you choose, but the farther from the "norm" that you make them, the more they will have to deal with their fellow members. They may be teased or mocked, and this is typically seen as camaraderie, not bullying, in the military/police/fire culture. Nicknames, call signs, or last names are typically used instead of first names. Readers love to see the dynamics within the brotherhood of these organizations.

CHAPTER 12

COMMON PITFALLS

Major disappointment, sir: You should know the difference in ranking, the structure of squads, platoons, and companies, or squads, units, and precincts in law enforcement. Firefighters, law enforcement agencies, and military will all have distinct structures and ranking systems, and that will differ across branches. This is one of the most commonly neglected details and it is SO easy to find this information. Local police and fire organizations are more likely to vary from jurisdiction to jurisdiction, but your familiarity with existing organizations will help you make informed decisions about your own fictional department.

That never happened: If you are writing about actual events, be sure to do your research! If you choose to deviate from the true events in minor details, or take creative license, be sure to write that in the author's note. Be aware of the timeline and what wars or operations the character might have participated in. This will inform you about what units your character might have served in. Readers can get behind suspending their knowledge of history for the sake of story, but they will very seldom tolerate poor research or lack of caring for the historical accuracy of a narrative.

Unexplained skills: Don't fall into the trap of assuming that military training or police/firefighting training makes your character an expert at all things tactical, investigative, or heroic. In real life "having military training" means the same thing as any other profession in the world; they're trained as specialists in one particular role (which hopefully they do well) and may not know all the details of the other roles, so consider what role your uniformed character is meant to fill and apply their due weaknesses everywhere else—or be sure to prepare a reason for their skill in other fields.

Unrealistic perspective: It's tempting to give your character a 50,000-foot view idealism. When in combat, under fire, or fighting a fire—the mentality is less idealistic and more survival of the team. These heroes are not just there to keep themselves alive and unharmed, they want to ensure the entire team makes it through. No man left behind. In the thick of battle, they aren't thinking of the big picture implications of the fight, just the moment-to-moment action. Keeping this perspective in mind will make your characters feel authentic and avoid any eye-roll moments where your character is pontificating on the implications of the mission rather than focusing on the job at hand.

Now, let's look a little closer at each subset of this character trope.

Men (and Women) In Uniform

FIREFIGHTER/EMT

LAW ENFORCEMENT

MILITARY

FIREFIGHTERS/EMTS

THIS TROPE FEEDS THE READER'S
DESIRE FOR BRAVE AND SELFLESS
HEROES

Be sure to read the general *Men and Women in Uniform* information. It also applies to this entry.

In these stories, at least one main character is a Firefighter or an Emergency Medical Technician (EMT). This could encompass both volunteers and full-time professionals, hailing from city or rural settings. The cast extends to wildland firefighters, including daring smokejumpers, and even dedicated arson investigators. These tales revolve around heroes and heroines characterized by their remarkable bravery, selflessness, and unyielding commitment to safeguarding lives and communities from the ravages of fires and emergencies.

Within the heart of these narratives lies the captivating world of firefighting and emergency response, where fire stations serve as hubs of action, intense rescue operations unfold, and the adrenaline-fueled environment is the norm. While the firefighting or EMT aspect is often central to the plot, its significance can vary.

The protagonists are propelled by an unshakeable sense of duty, camaraderie, and a resolute aspiration to bring about positive change in the lives of those they serve. They find themselves confronted by perilous circumstances that demand rapid thinking, physical prowess, and an unwavering well of courage. As they battle voracious flames and navigate treacherous rescues, their own inner battles and vulnerabilities come to the forefront.

What captivates readers is not only the valor and heroism of the characters but also the profound emotional dimension that emanates from facing life-and-death scenarios. Amidst the fierce trials, our heroes and heroines must also grapple with their own fears and insecurities.

WHY READERS LOVE IT

Firefighters embody the spirit of bravery, rushing fearlessly into danger to save lives and protect communities from the ravages of fire. In the realm of romantic fiction, these characters hold a special place, as they are universally admired and celebrated for their heroic endeavors.

One of the most endearing aspects of Firefighter romance is the admiration and appreciation society holds for firefighters. Unlike Military or Law Enforcement characters, Firefighters are met with near-universal adoration, as they represent the beacon of hope and salvation during crises. Their sole purpose is to save lives and property from the devastating effects of fire, embodying the essence of selflessness and service to others.

EMTs respond to medical emergencies, car accidents, and other life-threatening situations. These characters may share similarities with the Doctor/Medical Professional Trope, providing a unique blend of emergency medical expertise and heroic valor. Readers are drawn to the dynamic combination of a strong, protective hero who is also skilled in providing essential medical care.

In the world of Firefighter romance, readers find brave, loyal, and protective characters who are the epitome of selflessness.

Firefighters are heroes without exception, with little room for morally gray portrayals. Their unwavering dedication to saving lives and property ignites the reader's admiration and respect.

READER EXPECTATIONS

Firefighters are brave, loyal, and protective, but they can also tend to be adrenaline seekers or reckless—drawn to the thrill of facing danger head-on. They aren't expected to be as black and white as some of our other *Men in Uniform* characters, but these other dynamics beyond their heroic nature make for varied and interesting characters.

EMTs and Firefighters are also cool and calm in the face of chaos and danger. They are comfortable making decisions in the heat of the moment (pun intended!) and that confidence and sureness are attractive qualities you can highlight throughout your narrative.

These stories might include scenes at the fire station with the camaraderie and brotherhood of fellow firefighters, or scenes where you actually go with the main character into the heat of the fire, trying to save a building or a person. These stories shine in action-packed or emotional scenes where the Firefighter has the opportunity to save someone from peril.

Like most of the *Men in Uniform* tropes, the Firefighter trope lends itself to romantic suspense by the nature of the job. If your book is not suspenseful and features a firefighter, be sure to communicate that in the cover and blurb so you do not make promises for suspense that do not get fulfilled.

Don't get me wrong, you can get away with writing a Firefighter book without it being full of suspense and danger. There are other aspects of the firefighting life that you can use to meet the readers' expectation without crossing the line into suspense if that is not what you want to write. Lean into the community aspect of the small town or the brotherhood of the department. Highlight your wilderness firefighter's love of nature and desire to protect the land. Show the day-to-day life of a firefighter or EMT even if you don't take the reader into the fire enough to feel the flames.

COMMON PITFALLS

The skills gap: If your character has a specific skill, make sure their background is consistent for that particular skill. Firefighters can be employed in a variety of roles like EMTs, paramedics, wildland firefighters, and fire investigators. Don't expect your rookie firefighter to recognize arson or your urban firefighter to understand how to put out a wildfire while visiting a ranch in Oklahoma. Some firefighters are not trained as EMTs and some EMTs are not trained to fight fires, but some are.

I'm still human: Firefighters often face trauma and high-stress situations. Don't forget to address the emotional toll these experiences take on their mental health and relationships realistically. The demands of the firefighting profession can impact the characters' ability to nurture their romance, so be sure to portray their vulnerabilities, struggles, and moments of doubt to make them relatable and human.

LAW ENFORCEMENT

THIS TROPE FEEDS THE READER'S DESIRE FOR BRAVE AND CLEVER HEROES

Be sure to read the general *Men and Women in Uniform* information. It also applies to this entry.

Romance featuring Law Enforcement delves into the romantic entanglements and adventures of characters working on the force. These stories often feature protagonists who are police officers, detectives, FBI agents, or other professionals involved in maintaining law and order. The setting may include bustling urban landscapes, crime scenes, and police precincts, providing an atmospheric backdrop to the romance.

In Law Enforcement Officer (LEO) romances, the heroes and heroines are driven by a sense of justice, a commitment to protect their communities, and a desire to make a difference. They possess a strong moral compass and often find themselves faced with dangerous and thrilling situations. As they navigate the challenges of their demanding careers, they also grapple with personal conflicts, balancing their duty with their desires for love and companionship.

Members of law enforcement may form deep emotional connections with their partners, witnesses, or informants, requiring them to navigate the complexities of maintaining professionalism while being true to their feelings. The characters' sense of duty can lead to internal conflicts, making their personal journeys toward love and happiness as compelling as the thrilling cases they solve.

In Law Enforcement Officer romance, readers find a blend of action, suspense, and heartfelt emotion that captivates their hearts and keeps them engaged from the first page to the last. These stories offer a unique perspective on the power of love amidst the challenges and dangers of the law enforcement world, leaving readers eager to follow the romantic journey of these brave and passionate characters.

Law Enforcement at any level could fall into this category:

- Federal agent
  - FBI
  - Secret Service
  - CIA/Secret agent
  - US Marshal
  - Border Patrol
- Park/Forest ranger
- Sheriff
- Local police
- Security guard
- Bounty hunter
- Interpol
- Foreign police agencies

WHY READERS LOVE IT

The allure of LEO romances lies in the combination of intrigue, suspense, and passion. Readers are drawn to the tension between the characters' dedication to their work and their emotional vulnerabilities. The dynamics of power and trust play a significant role in these romances, as the heroes and heroines must confront their own fears and insecurities to open their hearts to love.

Readers of Law Enforcement romance are inherently drawn to the essence of the profession. They hold a profound admiration for characters engaged in the fight for good versus evil, where right prevails over wrong. The idea of protagonists fighting for justice, battling against criminal elements, and protecting the innocent resonates deeply with their sense of moral compass.

These readers seek heroes and heroines who epitomize integrity, bravery, and a deep-rooted commitment to serving and protecting their communities. Characters who uphold the law and make the tough choices for the greater good are celebrated, reflecting the reader's desire to witness the triumph of justice and the defeat of wrongdoing. This subset of readers seeks stories that celebrate the triumph of justice and honor, with morally upright heroes who stand as unwavering defenders of truth and righteousness.

These books dive into the emotional struggles and vulnerabilities of characters in this line of work. Beneath their tough exteriors, these heroes and heroines grapple with the psychological toll of their high-stress careers. Readers appreciate the depth of these characters, as they are portrayed as individuals with their own fears, traumas, and desires for love and companionship. The juxtaposition of their tough exterior with the tenderness of their romantic connections is what keeps readers coming back again and again.

READER EXPECTATIONS

When writing Law Enforcement characters, readers expect to see brains behind the badge. Law Enforcement heroes should be critical thinkers. They are constantly analyzing and cataloging information, almost subconsciously. These characters tend to have keen attention to detail (like that little freckle right at the nape of her neck that he is just dying to place a kiss on). How many times have you read a book and thought, "No way this dude notices that detail?" This is the trope to use all those minute features that your character *will* in fact notice, because he's trained to notice. This also makes these characters excel when there is a puzzle of some sort to solve.

In this trope, morally gray characters are not often found in the spotlight. Readers prefer protagonists who wholeheartedly choose right over wrong, even if it means facing personal challenges and sacrifices. A corrupt or crooked law enforcement officer is unlikely to find acceptance as a hero in these stories. Instead, readers desire characters whose dedication to justice is unwavering, who navigate complex ethical dilemmas with integrity, and who uphold their principles in the face of temptation and adversity.

It's difficult to avoid the suspense element in Law Enforcement stories, and there will almost always be a strong external force of conflict. It's not required, but it does give your character the chance to shine and show off all those hero characteristics readers love and expect. The character will be acutely aware of any risks, whether that is weather-related, locations of questionable safety, or situations that simply don't feel right. This gives your hero the opportunity to act—driving the story instead of simply reacting. Even if neither of the main characters are in any real danger for most of the story, give your Law Enforcement hero a chance to flex those protector muscles that readers love to see.

COMMON PITFALLS

The skills gap: Skills and experience gaps in law enforcement can come in many forms. Familiarity with various weapons or crimes is a big one. If your small-town sheriff is suddenly in the middle of a cartel murder with drug trafficking involved, that's going to be way outside his normal scope, and he will feel very out of his element. But if he happens to have recently moved from Los Angeles where he worked on the gang unit—perhaps he feels very equipped to protect his town from this new threat.

Inaccuracy: Accuracy and authenticity are essential in every trope and genre, but it is especially important to readers involving crime and law enforcement. Don't rely on what you see in movies and on television to give you an accurate depiction of police work and procedure. Plot elements, including police-related shootings, internal investigations, and reading of the Miranda rights, are commonly botched, much to the frustration of readers who have real-life knowledge or experience in law enforcement.

MILITARY

Be sure to read the general *Men and Women in Uniform* information. It also applies to this entry.

Military romance revolves around the love and relationships of characters connected to the military. These stories typically feature heroes or heroines who are active-duty service members, veterans, or individuals closely tied to military life.

The setting often includes military bases or deployments, and the plot typically revolves around the challenges faced by those serving in the armed forces, or of those who recently left active duty and are reintegrating into civilian life.

Military romances explore themes of sacrifice, resilience, and the bonds formed through shared experiences in times of conflict and camaraderie. The heroes and heroines in these stories navigate the complexities of love amidst the demands of duty, making for emotionally charged and heartwarming narratives that resonate with readers.

Some examples of Military units include:

- US Army
  - Green Berets
  - Delta Force
- US Navy

- o Navy SEALs
- US Air Force
- Coast Guard
- Marines
- Space Force
- Foreign military/special ops
  - o Royal Australian Air Force
  - o United Kingdom Special Forces
  - o British Army
  - o SAS British Special Forces
  - o Mossad
  - o French Foreign Legion

WHY READERS LOVE IT

Readers love being immersed in military culture. This subgenre provides a window into that world, a place where courage and dedication intertwine with the vulnerabilities of the human heart. Whether readers have personal ties to the military or not, the appeal of Military romance lies in its ability to transport them into a world of bravery, strength, and enduring love.

For those with a personal connection to the military, these stories hold a special place in their hearts. Military spouses and significant others find solace and understanding in the characters' experiences, as they mirror their own journey of love and resilience in the face of challenges unique to military life. The characters' sacrifices, separations, and unwavering commitment resonate deeply with these readers, creating a powerful connection that goes beyond the pages of the book. Military romance offers them a sense of community and understanding, a shared camaraderie with characters who navigate the complexities of military service and love.

On the other hand, readers with no personal connection to the military are drawn to Military romance for the escapism it offers. The allure of a strong Military hero, guided by a code of honor and courage, captivates the imagination. These heroes embody qualities of bravery, discipline, and selflessness that inspire admiration and intrigue. The Military setting provides a familiar yet distinct world, making it accessible for readers to immerse themselves in this realm of action and adventure. Through Military romance, they can vicariously experience the thrill of battle, the depth of emotions, and the triumph of love in the face of adversity.

Military romance sheds light on the human side of the military, offering a glimpse into the personal lives of soldiers beyond their uniforms and combat roles. These stories delve into the emotional struggles, fears, and vulnerabilities of Military characters, showing them not just as warriors but as individuals with dreams, hopes, and desires. The juxtaposition of bravery in the field and tenderness in love creates multifaceted characters that feel relatable and authentic, further strengthening the connection between readers and the story.

READER EXPECTATIONS

Military members face an intensity unseen in most other occupations. As a member of the armed forces, you are called upon to relinquish your individuality for the sake of the mission. This leaves us with heroes and heroines who possess a certain intensity themselves, and it leads to *charged* connections between your love interest. The military requires grit, submission to the greater good, boldness in the face of uncertainty and danger, and staying calm in the midst of the battle.

This produces nuanced characters who may have deep struggles, though they will be practiced at facing even the toughest situations with stability and assurance. They have a sense of duty and honor, and an even stronger sense of loyalty to those they consider in their inner circle.

For military readers in the US, there is an unspoken expectation of patriotism. Readers who are anti-military or unsupportive of veterans don't tend to pick up these books. So, while every service member knows that the service isn't perfect, you should avoid condemning the military except in the smallest of ways. With few exceptions, even service members who have left the service with scars tend to be protective of their experiences. Service in the military is not something most regret, nor would they openly disparage the organization. They may mock the paperwork or the time it takes for things to happen due to bureaucracy or inefficiency. They may groan about a tough commanding officer or recall a particular order they didn't want to carry out. But the overall tone readers expect from these characters is one of pride and respect for the organization they serve (or served.)

COMMON PITFALLS

Know what you write: Talk to active-duty service members or find resources from people who served during the time of your story. The military is constantly changing, from the procedures to the weapons to the uniforms. Many of these details can be easily found online at military websites, so be sure to look into these things before making assumptions in your writing. If you served, your own personal experience will be valuable, but if it is dated, be sure to account for changes.

Not created equal: Be aware of the subcultures and respect the differences of branches. The military branches are vastly different, from structure and ranking to locations to culture. The persona between a Marine grunt and an airman is bound to be incredibly different, and those who are familiar with each branch will recognize a lack of understanding almost immediately. Having a conversation with someone who served in the particular branch you are writing about, if not in a similar unit or squad, is a great start. You can often find veterans or military spouses in online communities who would be happy to provide feedback.

The skills gap: The skills gap for military is often related to weapons or equipment. A fighter pilot isn't likely to be able to hop into any random helicopter and fly it like an expert. A Marine intelligence officer probably won't be able to use a Remington 700 to take out a target at 1500 yards. Make sure their skills and background align, or create another reason why they possess the skill you need.

MEN (AND WOMEN) IN UNIFORM ADDITIONAL INFORMATION

COMMONLY PAIRED TROPES

Due to the heroic nature of their career, these character tropes are often paired with the situational trope of the Damsel in Distress or Protector. It affords the perfect opportunity for the Man in Uniform to use all of the skills and character attributes he has to save the female main character and fall in love all at the same time.

Local Police and Firefighters are often paired with the setting trope of Small Town, though a wildlands Firefighter might be a better pairing with a Ranch setting.

Don't allow this to limit you though. A hero with a military, law enforcement, or firefighter career or background is a wonderful layer to add to your character in many types of stories.

POTENTIAL WOUNDS

Being held captive
A traumatic brain injury
Battling a mental disorder (PTSD)
Losing a limb
Accidentally killing someone
Bearing the responsibility for many deaths
Cracking under pressure
Failing to save someone's life
Being disappointed by a role model
Being let down by a trusted organization

COMMON TRAITS

Heroic	Daredevil	Determined
Loyal	Macho	Courageous
Organized	Bold	Steadfast
Brave	Adventurous	Honorable
Selfless	Valiant	Protective

CHAPTER 13

MONEY, MONEY TROPES

THESE TROPES FEED THE READER'S DESIRE TO BE PROVIDED FOR AND ADORED/CHERISHED

Money is no object, but it can't buy them love.

This trope category includes everything from Billionaires to Celebrities (including famous Musicians) and Royalty or Regency characters.

Much of the appeal of these tropes lies in the larger-than-life fantasy: the idea that you can have anything your heart desires, including true love. Despite the criticism that this is a typically materialistic category, these stories really shine when they show that, in fact, true love is more valuable than any worldly possession or riches—that the adoration of one person can overshadow the adoration of thousands.

While the allure of this trope is the fantasy and mystery of a larger-than-life protagonist, you will hook your readers by making them relate to your characters on a strictly human level. Strip them of the fame, the castles, or the riches, and they are just a person looking for love and fulfillment.

We'll walk through these tropes individually, since they and the expectations/pitfalls are quite different. But the common thread is that of "money can't buy you love."

BILLIONAIRE/RICH GUY

CELEBRITY/ROCKSTAR/MUSICIAN

ROYALTY/REGENCY

BILLIONAIRE/RICH GUY

*THIS TROPE FEEDS THE READER'S
DESIRE TO BE WANTED BY SOMEONE
WHO HAS EVERYTHING*

In this trope, one (sometimes both) of the protagonists is a billionaire or wealthy beyond measure. These heroes are often (but not always) Alpha Males: strong, Type A, driven, assertive, and "in control" of their world. Even if they are not an Alpha Male, there is a special kind of confidence that comes with knowing that you can have anything you want with the swipe of a Black Card.

The crux of Billionaire romances lies in the imbalance of power, worldviews, or lived experience. Most often it's done as a wealthy man and a woman from humble beginnings, but that can be flipped, or it can even be done with two billionaire protagonists.

When both protagonists are coming from the same socioeconomic background, the trick is to create that imbalance elsewhere—old money versus new money, one who is passionate about their work and another who is a slave to the shareholders, etc.

No matter the circumstances, the power and the draw of these stories lie in overcoming that imbalance; at the heart, Billionaire romances are something of a Cinderella story. This imbalance creates the basis of the conflict and tension for the romance to unfold.

WHY READERS LOVE IT

No matter the current financial status of the average reader, they are surely not staring at nine zeroes in their bank account. The Billionaire (or other rich, wealthy main character) has near infinite resources, and that offers stability and comfort for the love interest, even if they fight against it with everything they have.

As one blogger put it, paying bills is sexy.

It's not just the allure of a bottomless expense account and extravagant dates. The fantasy fulfillment ultimately lies in the idea that a man who could have nearly anything or anyone at the snap of a finger would choose you—because you're special. Or the female protagonist is, anyway.

Readers love to enter this fantasy world where a powerful man will do anything for the woman he loves. He'll move mountains to protect her, care for her, and make her smile. And that's intoxicating.

The Billionaire is used to being in control of his world, and it's most often the heroine who enters and dashes his sense of control. While this initially may be a source of frustration for the Billionaire, once he decides to pursue the relationship, he is *all in*. Be sure to reveal why your billionaire is also drawn into the relationship, because ultimately, he must be willing to turn his world on its head in order to keep the one he loves; this means that your love interest must be a compelling and relatable character in her own right. Instant attraction is one thing, but by the midpoint or climax of the story, the hero needs to be able to articulate WHY the heroine is so special. What makes her different, and why she was able to get past his defenses?

READER EXPECTATIONS

We can't ignore the expectation of the Billionaire experience. What do we mean by this? These characters have more money than you can fathom. Extravagant gifts (bonus points if they're thoughtful) or destination dates will make your reader feel swept away in the romance of it all. These heroes won't even think about paying extra for convenience of deliveries, special arrangements, or paying for sold out tickets. He can't buy her love—and while he might know that in his heart, it isn't likely to keep him from showing her how he feels by spending some of his money on things to make her smile.

Rich heroes can also be a bit abrasive and utterly unrelatable though, so it is important that you don't shy away from the complexity and nuances of their character. Most often, it's this complexity and the enigma that draws the love interest in. For example, the reclusive billionaire who is the secret benefactor of a specific charity makes you want to uncover why. The nerdy tech billionaire who can command a boardroom but gets tongue tied around his new next-door neighbor has an endearing crack in his armor that the reader wants to uncover.

Be sure to incorporate the source of your character's wealth and how it affects their lifestyle and relationships. Do they need to maintain a certain reputation in order to keep mommy and daddy satisfied and keep the line of finances open? Is your CEO at the mercy of shareholders, big name clients, or board members of the various charities he supports? How does the lifestyle differ between the owner of a holding company and an outdoor brand?

Sometimes wealth provides a much-needed parachute for the protagonist or a loved one of the protagonist. How does that impact the relationship?

Basically, having money is going to impact the thoughts of your character in some way or another. Don't let them be a Billionaire in name only and ignore the impact of that on their actions and thoughts—or the way it will impact their love interest. It is quite likely that something a Billionaire wouldn't think twice about buying would be cataclysmic to your average Jane, even if she isn't destitute. Lean into that discomfort and reassure the reader that the love between the characters is stronger.

You can get away with a Billionaire who doesn't act "typical," especially if they are new to their fortune. Someone raised with wealth will think differently about it than someone who recently inherited or earned their fortune.

COMMON PITFALLS

Entitled heroes: If a Billionaire character is a little too comfortable with their status and wealth, they can come across as entitled. Don't make your hero so unlikeable that we can't root for him. However, a little tension between your lovers due to the spoils of privilege can make things interesting.

Conniving and gold-digger heroines: No one sympathizes with a woman who is viciously targeting a man for his fortune. If she's entering a marriage of convenience, make sure she has good reason to. Reluctance on her part is a pretty sure-fire way to make sure she doesn't seem conniving.

Arrogance to a fault: It's okay to admit it, we all like a little swagger from time to time. And if your watch costs more than my minivan, you've probably earned the right to be a little cocky. A little naive arrogance can be overlooked for a hero with a heart of gold, but a jerk is a jerk no matter how many dollar signs he writes next to his name. And we have to be able to root for him as the person behind the swagger.

Manipulation: Avoid manipulation on the part of either protagonist. When it comes off as if the hero is using his money or other resources to manipulate or "buy her love," it feels like almost an abuse of power.

COMMONLY PAIRED TROPES

The Billionaire is often paired with tropes that engage with the type of situations that extraordinary amounts of money can provide or require. Marriage of Convenience, Damsel in Distress, and Playboy are a few examples where the Billionaire's money either enables or forces the storyline.

Alternately, tropes that humanize the excessively rich character such as Widow, Single Parent, Girl Next Door, or Rags to Riches are other common pairings. Another example would be pairing the Billionaire trope with the Hidden or Mistaken Identity (often referred to as Secret Billionaire). These Billionaires long to be treated as a normal person—even if it's just for a little while.

Enemies to Lovers is a common pairing because it plays on the power dynamics and clashes that occur when someone does not simply defer to the inherent power and influence of their wealth. Internal character tropes like Alpha Male, Grump, or Lone Wolf are combined with Billionaire to provide additional depth to the character and give him a natural repelling force for any love interest.

POTENTIAL WOUNDS

Cracking under pressure
Making a very public mistake

BILLIONAIRE/RICH GUY

Poor judgement leading to unintended consequences
Experiencing poverty
A sibling's betrayal
Infidelity
Living in an emotionally repressed household
A parent's divorce

COMMON TRAITS

Confident	Generous	Arrogant
Spoiled	Protective	Untrusting
Out of touch	Ambitious	Self centered
Insensitive	Intelligent	Hard working

CELEBRITY/ROCK STAR/MUSICIAN

THESE TROPES FEED THE READER'S DESIRE FOR A LARGER-THAN-LIFE HERO

Celebrity and Rock Star romances both involve one very famous person (or Rock Star/Musician) falling in love with a more or less average person. The characters in these books may be movie stars, social media influencers, mega popular artists or writers, or any other entertainment figure.

Rock Star romances tend to be a bit more nuanced given the Bad Boy and rock and roll persona. Romances in these two categories are all about overcoming the challenges of a very public life in order to make the relationship work. Like any romance, these categories will ultimately require sacrifice and a great deal of effort on the part of your protagonists in order to achieve their happily ever after.

Celebrity and Rock Star romances showcase unique circumstances arising from the nature of their fame. In the celebrity world, reputation and image management play a crucial role in shaping relationships. Paparazzi and media attention can lead to misunderstandings, while fans' adoration can create tension and jealousy. On the other hand, Rock Star romances introduce elements of music, touring, and groupies, challenging the protagonists' commitment to each other amidst a chaotic and fast-paced lifestyle.

As authors explore the creative and musical attributes of their characters, they should avoid falling into stereotypes. Not every musician is plagued by depression, nor is every celebrity fame hungry. Instead, delve into the complexities of your characters, painting them as multifaceted individuals with dreams, fears, and desires beyond their fame.

WHY READERS LOVE IT

Celebrity and Rock Star romances place a heavy emphasis on the idea of fantasy fulfillment for the reader. Readers are transported to glamorous settings, backstage parties, and red-carpet events, providing a vicarious experience of the high life.

Celebrity romances are popular for the same reason that tabloids are popular—unbelievable people doing unbelievable things causes even the most reluctant reader to turn their heads. These stories are filled with drama and turmoil, the protagonists are messy and nuanced, and the experience is both enchanting and entertaining. Your hero may intentionally make time for love amidst the chaos or love may find them when they least expect it.

At the end of the day—these are just people, like you and me. Taking the reader "behind the scenes" with their favorite movie star and fulfilling the idea that maybe they would fall in love with normal, everyday Jane is the ultimate daydream.

READER EXPECTATIONS

Fame is the name of the game in this trope. Good and bad, this fame carries major implications on your story. Lack of privacy is a major source of conflict, from tabloids and gossip rags to managers and publicists, or even invasive fans. And you can't ignore the conflicts of demanding schedules and long stints of travel.

But fame also has its privileges. There might be exclusive events and after parties. Your characters might rub shoulders with other famous characters or have the opportunity to support charitable causes near and dear to their heart.

In a Rock Star romance your protagonist is either adored or hated (but still followed) by millions. Their stories will often include a troubled protagonist with a Bad Boy personality, but be sure to redeem this character so that readers can connect and empathize with your hero, ultimately rooting for the success of the relationship. These stories could also feature a famous musician who feels very down-to-earth, such as the small-town boy turned country music star. Strong chemistry between your hero and heroine will help to ground your reader, but the Rock Star is not going to focus in on the heroine in a sea of fifteen thousand fans—at night, with the lights in his eyes—unless you give him a reason to.

As with Celebrity romances, you will want to cultivate chemistry between protagonists, but Rock Star romances will almost always feature magnetic heroes with a healthy dose of angst in order to satisfy that Rock Star character. For these characters, music is typically the medium for healing and redemption, with songs or grand gesture performances used to demonstrate just how deep the connection goes, and just what they are willing to sacrifice for love.

COMMON PITFALLS

Outrageous circumstances: While some fantasy fulfillment is desired and celebrities are known for doing the most outrageous things, authors should be careful not to make these stories *too* unbelievable (even if real life often is). Readers will suspend their disbelief to some extent for these stories, but you still need to make them realistic.

Vocation: Your character didn't achieve their fame by being lazy, even if there was a significant amount of luck involved. If they are currently working, you'll need to show them on set, at rehearsal, practicing lines or writing the songs that made them famous.

Romance: Don't make the romance too easy to obtain in these stories. There are significant forces trying to keep your characters apart, despite the money and status. It could be prejudice, fear, or external forces (such as a greedy agent or producer)—but the challenges of your characters cannot be minimized if you truly want your reader to believe in and root for the couple.

COMMONLY PAIRED TROPES

Celebrity and Rock Star romances are often written with tropes that allow the Celebrity to fall for a "normal" partner. Whether that is the Celebrity looking for love on a Reality TV show, or using tropes like Nanny or Workplace romance to allow for enough interaction that the main character has the opportunity to fall for the love interest.

Alternately, these characters are also commonly paired with tropes that highlight the fact that they are people just like us, with pasts and family ties that aren't so different. Second Chance, Coming Home, Small Town, All Grown Up, and Brother's Best Friend are some common tropes that bring these spotlighted heroes into a less intimidating perspective.

POTENTIAL WOUNDS

Being treated as property
Being stalked
Being so beautiful it's all people see
Choosing to not be involved in a child's life

Caving to peer pressure
Making a very public mistake
Being the victim of a vicious rumor
Infidelity
Being raised by a narcissist
Being raised by parents who loved conditionally
Growing up in the public eye

COMMON TRAITS

Ambitious	Conceited	Rebellious
Creative	Hardworking	Flamboyant
Thoughtful	Private	Unpredictable
Bold	Charismatic	Glamourous
Arrogant	Confident	Eccentric

ROYALTY/REGENCY

THESE TROPES FEED THE READER'S DESIRE TO SEE LOVE OVERCOME THE RULES OF ANY SOCIETY

When writing using a Royalty or Regency trope, at least one of your protagonists must be descended from royalty or nobility.

As you might expect, the Royalty trope will include kings, queens, princes, and princesses, but it may also include emperors, sheiks, or a sultan. If you're writing historical romance, this may also include Rana of India, Kaiser, Tsar, Pharaoh, or Caesar.

Regency romance is a romance subgenre that takes place in high society England during the early 19th century. This group is known as the ton and includes the peerage, aristocracy, and well-connected, wealthy families. We will get more into the historical aspect of Regency romance in the *Settings* volume of our *Trope Encyclopedia* series, but for now we will focus on the character requirements. Regency heroes and heroine may include the duke/duchess, marquess/marchioness, earl/countess, viscount(ess), and baron(ess).

Depending on the era you are writing in, some of the sources of conflict for your royals may include royal duties, media attention, reputation, gossip, need for an heir, family pressures, and political conflict or alliances. The love of your protagonists will largely be forged through these trials. Most often in a Royal romance, the deepest conflict will originate from external pressures that create some kind of internal or relational wound.

WHY READERS LOVE IT

Royalty romance, like other *Money, Money* tropes, thrives on the allure of fulfilling fantasies. Readers are transported to a world of opulence and grandeur, experiencing stories and adventures they could only imagine in their wildest dreams or beloved books. The setting of palaces, lavish comforts, enchanting balls, exquisite gowns, and a retinue of servants tantalizes the senses. Embrace these elements and let them shine, allowing them to whisk readers away to a realm of elegance and extravagance. However, remember that the heart of the story lies in the captivating romance between the hero and heroine, so let their love story take center stage.

The ultimate satisfaction in royalty romance comes from the powerful notion that love knows no boundaries. Class or social standing become inconsequential in the face of true love. Readers revel in the idea that love can triumph against all odds, even in the face of significant opposition. The courage to defy norms and break societal rules for the sake of love resonates deeply with readers, as they witness characters navigating the complexities of choosing love over duty (or perceived duty). This recurring theme adds depth and emotional resonance to the story, leaving readers with a heartwarming sense of fulfillment in the happily ever after.

READER EXPECTATIONS

In the enchanting world of Royalty and Regency romance, certain elements hold a special place in readers' hearts, and meeting these expectations is key to crafting a captivating tale.

Whether modern-day or historical, readers relish the opulence and associated with royal wardrobes. The stark contrast between a royal's couture and a pauper's humble attire adds an element of wonder and excitement. Very few women have the knowledge or experience of a wardrobe worthy of royalty, and if your royal is falling for a pauper, it will all be new to her as well! Let them be overwhelmed by the couture, the glamour, and the world-class jewels that your prince or duke is sure to shower her with.

High-society events, such as balls and gatherings, are a staple in these romances, providing ample opportunities for lavish gowns, dazzling jewels, and ballroom dancing. Alongside these grand occasions, witty banter and clever dialogue, dashing heroes and relatable heroines should be prominent. Readers read them expecting the delightful subtext of a conversation laced with double meaning and careful insults—or compliments that push the boundaries of familiarity. The art of polite conversation, carefully masking emotions and intentions, adds depth to the characters' interactions.

The rigid stratification of society significantly influences the dynamics between characters. The titles and social standing of the protagonists play a crucial role in determining the acceptability of their relationships. Overcoming these class barriers becomes a central theme, and the challenges they face contribute to the richness of their love story. The titles of your character will make a great deal of difference in the way your characters relate—for example, a duke choosing to marry a lady will make plenty of sense to their peers, whereas a duke falling for the daughter of a baron may raise some eyebrows. Although you will read plenty of Regency romance that reads more like a Cinderella tale, you will be much more successful in fulfilling your reader by portraying the difficulties of breaking societal norms. The more challenging the obstacles faced by the couple, the more satisfying the happily ever after will be.

There will be much fodder for gossip and scandal, and your characters may feel immense pressure to conform or rebel against these norms—or maintain a delicate balance between the two. Be aware that in Regency romance, female virtue and dependence are emphasized, and a woman who fails to maintain her virtue or find a suitable match (marrying a man of *status*) would be scandalized. Given the entitlement of males in the ton, your male protagonist is much more likely to get away with breaking societal norms, and their status will allow them to be sought after anyway.

Royalty romance is similar to Regency in many ways, with class stratification and society events. Additional elements also come into play, such as fish-out-of-water scenarios, arranged marriages, and strong family ties. Cultural world-building and the inclusion of politics, warfare, and intrigue enrich the narrative, immersing readers in a realm of grandeur and complexity.

Overall, fulfilling reader expectations in Royalty and Regency romance involves artfully weaving a tapestry of fashion, societal norms, class barriers, and cultural intricacies. The portrayal of characters' struggles and triumphs amid these elements creates a captivating love story that resonates with readers, leaving them spellbound by the allure of royalty and the elegance of regency.

COMMON PITFALLS

Historical accuracy: In the world of Regency romance, attention to historical accuracy is essential, particularly when it comes to language, titles, hierarchy, and forms of address. Readers are well-versed in the period, and you must be too. Familiarize yourself with the intricacies of the peerage system and the appropriate dialect and slang terms, but remember to use them sparingly. A touch of historical flavor should enhance the story without overwhelming or confusing the reader.

Cardboard characters: To captivate readers further, break away from the traditional mold of stuffy heroes and heroines. Embrace the creative freedom to build a fictional kingdom with diverse personalities among the aristocracy. Not all nobility or royals need to be rigid or pretentious; explore different character traits within the aristocratic frame. For lower ranks among the peerage or middle class, give your heroes distinct and appealing attributes, setting them apart from higher-ranking nobility who might be more sought-after by those seeking social advancement.

Too much swoon: While literal swooning and fainting were once considered customary in Regency settings, modern readers appreciate strong and resilient heroines. Portray women as tough and capable, showcasing their strength in the face of challenges. Balance historical accuracy with the empowering portrayal of female characters, ensuring that they remain captivating and assertive throughout the narrative.

COMMONLY PAIRED TROPES

Royalty and Regency are a playground for tropes, and there is a bit more wiggle room for unbelievable situations, such as a prince hiding his identity or an archaic law that requires an heir to marry by a certain age. You are likely to have Opposites Attract or Enemies to Lovers far more often than Friends to More alongside this trope. Co-ed friendships were especially rare in the Regency period, and chaperones were almost always nearby if socializing was in mixed company. Forbidden Romance is a popular combination. Your Regency or Royalty hero may also take on additional character tropes like Lone Wolf, Rake, or Protector.

POTENTIAL WOUNDS

A learning disability
A physical disfigurement
Declaring bankruptcy
Failing to do the right thing
Making a very public mistake
Being falsely accused of a crime
Being rejected by one's peers
Misplaced loyalty
Being raised by neglectful parents
Being sent away as a child
Having parents who favored one child over another

COMMON TRAITS

Leadership	Demure	Witty
Confident	Determined	Elegant
Well mannered	Sensible	Graceful
Responsible	Honorable	Regal
Headstrong	Clever	Diplomatic

CHAPTER 14

TOUGH GUY TROPES

THESE TROPES APPEAL TO THE READER'S DESIRE TO REDEEM AND SOFTEN EVEN THE MOST HEAVILY-GUARDED HEART

Consider these heroes onions—layer by layer the love interest will uncover the tenderness and vulnerability beneath the hardened exterior as the reader slowly falls for him. (Wait...did we get that backward?) You will find no shortage of Alphas among these heroes, but don't let that fool you into thinking they're all the same. The details and reader expectations of each trope should highlight the differences and bring your individual tough guy to life.

It's worth noting that most of these tropes are written overwhelmingly in the steamy category. Clean authors might take advantage of this underserved niche, but they should understand that they are likely to catch a fair number of steamy readers, and this may affect ratings and feedback when certain aspects of the trope differ from what they're used to.

Be advised: if you are bothered by the use or any combination of the words *rugged*, *fierce*, or *masculine*, you may want to proceed with caution.

BODYGUARD

HIGHLANDER

PIRATE

WOODSMAN/LUMBERJACK

VIKING

BODYGUARD

THIS TROPE FEEDS THE READER'S DESIRE TO BE PROTECTED AND WORTH BREAKING THE RULES FOR

Bodyguard romance revolves around the relationship between a professional bodyguard and their client. In these stories, the bodyguard is tasked with protecting the protagonist from various threats, be it physical danger, stalking, or other forms of harm. The dynamics of this genre often involve an imbalance of authority and high-stakes situations, making it a compelling and thrilling reading experience.

The bodyguard character is typically depicted as strong, skilled, and highly competent in their role. They exude a sense of authority and protectiveness, which appeals to readers seeking a hero with a blend of ruggedness and vulnerability. Because of the assuredness of these characters, the Bodyguard may share several similarities with heroes in the *Passion and Competence* trope category. The client may vary in personality and background, ranging from a powerful public figure to an ordinary individual caught in extraordinary circumstances.

While the Bodyguard character can be an unofficial arrangement, the true power of the trope lies in the dynamics that are formed because it is a working relationship. It is more than a Protector trope—the Bodyguard trope is a unique combination of Workplace Romance, Forbidden Love, Boss/Employee, Man (or Woman) in Uniform, and Protector.

WHY READERS LOVE IT

The dynamic between the Bodyguard and the client adds an element of excitement and tension to Bodyguard romance. Readers are drawn to the idea of a strong, capable, and fiercely protective hero who dedicates himself to keeping the protagonist safe. Any good Bodyguard knows that he must protect the client at any cost, and a hero who is willing to sacrifice his life for the heroine wins automatic brownie points with readers. This sense of safety and guardianship allows the heroine to lower her guard, leading to intimate and emotionally charged moments between the characters.

Even if your Bodyguard doesn't have to sacrifice his life or physical health for the heroine, he may run the risk of having to sacrifice his livelihood for the relationship. The nature of the bodyguard-client relationship often makes romance feel off limits, especially if there are rules against fraternization or emotional involvement. These stories typically require the Bodyguard and the person being protected to spend a significant amount of time together, often in close quarters, which allows for emotional intimacy to develop and undeniable chemistry.

Bodyguard romance often includes elements of suspense, action, and danger, making it a thrilling and immersive reading experience. The characters face external threats and must rely on each other to navigate through perilous situations, adding depth to the narrative and keeping readers on the edge of their seats. These situations test the characters' emotional fortitude and force them to confront their fears and vulnerabilities. The bodyguard's protective nature and the love interest's (sometimes unwilling) reliance on the bodyguard create opportunities for emotional intimacy and growth, allowing readers to witness the characters' development and transformation throughout the story.

186

READER EXPECTATIONS

The Bodyguard (whether male or female) should embody the qualities of a skilled and powerful professional. Readers expect a hero who is physically capable, emotionally invested in his role, and fiercely protective of the client. The hero's dedication to his/her duty should be evident, and their loyalty to the client should form a significant part of the romance. Not that the client and the protectee are not always the same person. Perhaps a billionaire CEO hired the bodyguard to protect his young daughter—the conflicting desires between the CEO and his daughter will create a struggle within the Bodyguard to resist his growing feelings in order to carry out his assigned duties.

The heroine should be a well-developed character with their own strengths and vulnerabilities. Readers want a love interest who is relatable and can hold their own, even in dangerous situations. Their growth and emotional journey, influenced by the connection with the Bodyguard, should be integral to the story's development.

The romance should showcase the gradual and organic development of an emotional connection between the Bodyguard and the client. Readers seek a love story that goes beyond physical attraction, where trust, respect, and emotional intimacy play a crucial role. Readers want the thrill of characters navigating the complexities of their feelings while grappling with the potential consequences of their emotional involvement. Bodyguard romances are a perfect opportunity for slow burn romance to really shine.

This is one character trope that relies heavily on suspense elements to truly satisfy readers. Suspense, danger, and action drive the characters to face challenging and life-threatening situations. The Bodyguard's protective role and the client's vulnerability to threats should be central to the narrative.

COMMON PITFALLS

Superhero skills: In some Bodyguard romances, the hero's role as a protector may border on unrealistic, making him a near-invincible and superhuman figure. While a degree of strength and competence is expected, exaggerating these qualities can make the character less relatable and the romance less believable. Striking a balance between realism and romance is crucial to keep the story grounded and emotionally resonant.

Lack of professionalism: In some Bodyguard romances, the hero's professionalism and dedication to his duty may take a backseat to the romantic plot. While the romance is the central focus, it is essential to maintain the integrity of the Bodyguard's role. Readers may be disappointed if the hero's competence as a protector is compromised by becoming too emotionally involved or neglecting his responsibilities.

Lack of realistic threats: In a Bodyguard romance, the presence of threats and danger adds tension and excitement. However, if the threats feel contrived or lack authenticity, it can weaken the impact of the romance. The obstacles the characters face should feel plausible and have genuine stakes to maintain readers' investment in the story.

Ignoring emotional aftermath: The high-stress and dangerous situations characters face in Bodyguard romances can have significant emotional repercussions. Failing to address the emotional aftermath of traumatic events can make the story feel superficial and dismissive of the characters' struggles. It's essential to delve into their emotional journeys and provide a realistic portrayal of the impact of their experiences.

COMMONLY PAIRED TROPES

The Bodyguard trope is most commonly paired with tropes that make a "hired protector" plausible and necessary. This could be Royalty, Rags to Riches, Celebrity/Musician or other *Money, Money* tropes. It also pairs well with tropes that have some inherent vulnerability of the heroine built in, such as Damsel in Distress, Single Parent, and Widow (especially in historical romance).

The Bodyguard may also be Law Enforcement on a protective detail (such as a US Marshal or Secret Service). In these cases, especially with US Marshals, it is not uncommon to see this trope paired with tropes such as Amnesia or Secret Identity.

POTENTIAL WOUNDS

Failing to save someone's life
Poor judgement leading to unintended consequences
Accidentally killing someone
Cracking under pressure
Being unfairly blamed for someone's death
Being let down by a trusted organization
Misplaced loyalty

COMMON TRAITS

Loyal	Committed	Disciplined
Protective	Stoic	Resourceful
Vigilant	Observant	Resolute
Strong	Reliable	Trustworthy
Skilled	Fearless	Dedicated

HIGHLANDER

*THIS TROPE FEEDS THE READER'S
DESIRE FOR SCOTLAND. LITERALLY
JUST SCOTLAND.*

The Highlander trope features a story set in Scotland, almost always in the mountains, forests, or royal courts of the Highlands. Some Scottish romances with characters who hail from the Lowlands may sneak into this category, but they won't necessarily lend themselves to the same history or culture because these areas were settled by quite different people groups. The typical Highlander romance features strong heroes with a sense of loyalty and honor, and heroines who are spirited and independent.

The Highlander is strong, honorable, and protective, with a fierce loyalty to their clan and a deep sense of pride in their Scottish heritage. As a note, this trope most often portrays a Scottish hero, but there is some flexibility with the heroine—she may be a Highlander, a Lowlander, or an outlander. Whatever the case, one of the love interests is likely from the Highlands. These heroes have a wild and free spirit that draws readers in and are somewhat unconventional or even rebellious in their thinking—in many ways a mix between the Alpha Male and Bad Boy. These heroes may be unafraid to challenge authority or tradition, even as they root their identity in it. They may be skilled warriors, hunters, or craftsmen, with a deep connection to the land and its traditions, and possess the skills and strength necessary to survive in the harsh and rugged Scottish landscape.

The history of Scotland, including the ongoing struggles between the Highlanders and the English (such as in the Wars of Independence and the Jacobite Rebellion), may also feature prominently in the plot. Because of this, one of the most common themes in Highlander romances is the clash of cultures. Whether it's between feuding clans or a love interest who is from a different region, the Highlander takes great pride in his culture and will almost certainly lay down his life for his clan. This requires the hero and heroine to overcome their differences to find love and happiness together. Other common elements include battles, feuds, and political intrigue, as well as a strong emphasis on family and community.

Though this trope is growing in popularity among contemporary readers, it has been almost exclusively used in historical romance in the past, and most readers will automatically associate the Highlander trope with a historical setting. When used in contemporary, this trope should still reflect, the strong, honorable and loyal heroes of old.

WHY READERS LOVE IT

Readers who gravitate toward Highlander romance novels do so for the sense of adventure and escapism they provide. These readers *love* Scotland for its rugged beauty and its rich history and culture, just as they love the rugged, loyal, Alpha heroes who dwell there.

The setting of a Highlander romance often plays a central role in the story, especially in historical, with the mountainous landscape and the traditions and customs of the Scottish-Gaelic people providing a rich backdrop for the narrative. We will cover the Scotland Highlands trope in more depth in *Volume 4: Settings*, but the importance of the setting is essentially equal to the Highlander hero for many readers.

This trope can also work when pulling the Highlander from his comfort zone and sending him off somewhere else. The trick when doing this is to highlight the differences in culture and customs to give the reader glimpses of the Highlander's homeland. When it comes down to it, these readers want the Scottish essence to permeate these stories, and that should come through in the memories, personality, habits, and customs of your Highlander character.

In addition to their physical prowess, Highlander heroes often possess a strong moral code and sense of honor. They are typically loyal to their clan and their family, willing to fight and even die for those they love. This sense of heroism and selflessness is attractive to readers, even if their moral code is different from that of the modern-day reader.

Highlander heroes are also often depicted as having a deep emotional and romantic side. The Highlander is fiercely protective of their love interests, willing to do anything to keep them safe and happy. They may be passionate and intense in their love, expressing their feelings with a raw and powerful honesty.

READER EXPECTATIONS

Setting and historical accuracy are a huge draw for readers of Highland romances novels. It not only sets the scene but adds a level of authenticity to the narrative that highlights and provides context to the attributes of your Highlander hero.

The passion and pride inherent in the Highlander character easily lends themselves to battles between clans and outside forces, as

Highlanders struggle to maintain power and control over their territories.

While most dialects are written with only a sprinkle of specific pronunciation and vernacular language, this is one category where you are likely to encounter a much more prominent dialect. Because readers of these stories are looking for the full immersion experience, they may find a mere sprinkling of Scottish brogue to feel unnatural or unrealistic. Just be cautious that you *dinna* make it so heavy that readers stumble over it. If you have difficulty reading dialogue out loud, your reader will likely have a hard time reading it.

Highlander romance novels tend to feature complex and independent heroines who are not afraid to challenge traditional gender roles. These heroines are often as strong and capable as their Highlander counterparts and can hold their own. While the Damsel in Distress is a common trope here, playing on the protective instincts and sense of justice for the hero, weakness was frowned upon—even among the Highland women.

COMMON PITFALLS

Toxic masculinity: Highlander romance often features strong and dominant heroes, but be cautious not to glorify toxic masculinity. Avoid portraying aggressive, controlling, or chauvinistic traits in the hero. Instead, focus on his honorable and protective nature, showcasing qualities that empower and respect the heroine. While many older Highlander romances may include these qualities in a hero, even heroes who violate the heroine before wooing her into submission, this kind of characterization will almost certainly make your novel feel outdated.

Weak or helpless heroines: Balance the power dynamic between the hero and heroine. Avoid creating heroines who are entirely dependent on the hero or too naive to navigate the world around them. Empower the heroine with strengths and qualities that complement the hero's abilities.

Historical representation: Highlander romance is often set in historical Scotland, and it's essential to research and present an accurate depiction of the time and culture. Be mindful of anachronisms and avoid projecting modern values and perspectives onto antiquated characters and settings.

COMMONLY PAIRED TROPES

Tropes that highlight the toughness and strength of our Highlander heroes are commonly paired. This could be placing the Highlander in a Bodyguard role or another method of him helping a Damsel in Distress.

Clan dynamics also lead to circumstances such as Arranged Marriage, Marriage of Convenience, and Enemies to Lovers where the characters must overcome their prejudice to embrace their feelings. This may or may not be in the context of Forbidden Love, as characters from rival clans or different social classes fall in love despite the odds against them.

The use of Time Travel is also relatively common in Highlander romance, especially since the popularity of Diana Gabaldon's novel, *Outlander*.

POTENTIAL WOUNDS

Bearing the responsibility for many deaths
Failing to save someone's life

HIGHLANDER

Poor judgement leading to unintended consequences
An abuse of power
Being forced to leave one's homeland
Living through civil unrest
Infidelity
A parent's abandonment or rejection
Witnessing violence at a young age
A child dying on one's watch
Having to kill to survive

COMMON TRAITS

Strong	Proud	Passionate
Masculine	Skilled	Respectful
Rugged	Protective	Confident
Honorable	Chivalrous	Adventurous
Loyal	Courageous	Traditional

PIRATE

THIS TROPE FEEDS THE READER'S DESIRE FOR ADVENTURE AND EXCITING HEROES

Pirate romances can be set in medieval through contemporary times (though modern-day pirates will probably lack many of the other alluring aspects of this genre). A solid majority of these stories are set during the Golden Age of Piracy, between about 1650 and 1750.

These romances feature seafaring explorers, or even criminals, as the hero, and sometimes the heroine. Though, the romanticized version of the pirate is more akin to a Robinhood-type hero—with right motives, despite their otherwise questionable actions.

Pirate romance novels may take place in unique and exotic settings, including pirate ships sailing across stormy seas and raiding exotic Caribbean islands. They may also be set in the British Isles or the Mediterranean. For both characters and readers alike, these exotic locations promise to quench their wanderlust and lead to discovery. The setting adds to the overall allure and excitement of the story. But we'll cover those aspects more in the *Romance Writer's Encyclopedia Volume 4: Settings*.

As the chapter title suggests, this trope features tough heroes, but the heroines of these stories are built of equally stern stuff. These characters tend to be independent, with no time, interest, or need for love. However, they meet their match in the heroines of this niche. Pirate romance novels often feature strong, independent heroines who defy societal norms and take charge of their own lives and destinies.

WHY READERS LOVE IT

Pirate novels captivate readers with a thrilling blend of adventure, danger, and romance set against the backdrop of the high seas.

Readers are drawn to heroes who are brave, adventurous, and capable. They often have unique, quirky personalities (Captain Jack Sparrow, anyone?), and there is a fair bit of humor in the dialogue. The daring nature of these Pirate heroes is captured in their willingness to forego comfort and physical safety in pursuit of adventure and the hope of discovering fortune and treasure.

Typically, the Pirate character of these romances is the hero, but it can also be the heroine as captain of the ship or serving as a member of the crew—and she should be portrayed as being no less fierce than her male counterparts. Readers love to see these women hold their own and embrace their strength.

The love interests are brave, resourceful, and quick-witted, even if they are in the position of being "rescued" by pirates and at the mercy of the ship's captain. These heroines are not afraid to challenge the patriarchal norms of their time, and they often do so in bold and unconventional ways that endears readers.

READER EXPECTATIONS

The biggest unspoken expectation of these stories is that they are equally about adventure or excitement and romance. If these stories are written with a slower pace, readers of this trope will likely put the book down and not finish it. Setting your Pirate character onboard a ship and rocking the story into motion isn't enough for a true fan of these stories. They want to be in the action—complete with sword fights, treacherous voyages, daring escapes, rescues, and the discovery of fortune. These novels need to offer plenty of excitement and adventure to meet the reader's desires.

As with most of the *Tough Guy* tropes, the intense, action-packed scenes should be balanced by more intimate moments of romance and emotional connection with the characters. These larger-than-life heroes will be made to battle against all odds to find love, treasure, and a place in history.

Another theme often explored in Pirate romance novels is the idea of duty. Duty to the crew was of utmost importance, and individuals who shirked their responsibility were often punished harshly. Pirate captains earned the respect of their crew by keeping them alive, out of the grasp of their enemies (including the Navy), and demonstrating their skill in navigating the seas. Pirate romance novels may feature characters who must fulfill a duty to avenge a loved one or protect their crew from harm.

The age-old saying, "there is no honor among thieves" is only partly true when it comes to these novels. While the very existence of pirate crews usually results from mutiny against a cruel or weak captain, these men held to a strict code of honor and in many ways were very democratic. Treasure was distributed equally among the crew, and any rules and decisions were typically subject to a vote. The characterization of your Pirate should reflect this complex and nuanced morality.

The key value to demonstrate in Pirate fiction is that pirate culture placed a heavy importance on the good of the majority. In some cases, that meant mutiny or disobedience against the ship's captain. Pirate romance novels may feature characters who must choose between loyalty to their crew and personal gain, or who must navigate complicated alliances and betrayals in order to achieve their goals. When their pursuit of the love interest comes at the expense of their crew, this is bound to create intense personal and relational conflict.

It's not unusual for these stories to have hints of mythology and folklore. We cover this more in the settings volume of the *Romance Writer's Encyclopedia*, but due to the superstitious nature of the cultures, your characters are likely influenced by a widespread belief in omens or nautical superstitions.

It is worth noting that this trope sometimes involves a hero who is actually a privateer, and not an actual pirate. While many of the cultural elements and characterization will remain true for these privateer characters, it is important to recognize that these figures had a somewhat better reputation than their criminal counterparts, only attacking enemy ships and acting as a sort of freelance navy on behalf of their homeland. For more information on the differences between pirates and privateers, we encourage you to check out Mike Rendell's book *Pirates and Privateers in the 18th Century: The Final Flourish*.

COMMON PITFALLS

Glamorizing violence and piracy: Pirates are often associated with brutality and, while it would be unrealistic to completely shy away from this, your readers will have a difficult time connecting with and rooting for the happily ever after of a brutal and violent swashbuckler. Instead, focus on the hero's sense of justice and honor.

Non-consensual relationships: Consent is crucial in any romance story. Avoid romanticizing or normalizing non-consensual relationships, especially in scenarios where power dynamics could be uneven. Instead, focus on building relationships based on mutual respect, trust, and understanding between the hero and the heroine.

The relationship between these characters may change from outright hostility to intimacy, but that should not extend to the physical relationship in clean romance.

Lack of realism: While escapism is a key factor in enjoying Pirate romance novels, some scenarios may still feel too far-fetched or unrealistic for readers, particularly if they include improbable scenarios or exaggerated personalities. In order to balance out the extraordinary feats and adventures, lean into the nuances of your character and don't prioritize adventure and exoticism over well-developed characters and relationships.

COMMONLY PAIRED TROPES

Pirate romances are most commonly paired with Damsel in Distress, giving the character an opportunity to show their kindness and compassion in an environment where it is uncommon. These romances also feature Enemies to Lovers, and Opposites Attract, as the heroine fights her attraction for the hero who does not meet her standards of virtue or morality.

Because Pirates exist outside the law, their romantic entanglements are often perceived as forbidden or taboo. This Forbidden Love dynamic adds an extra layer of intensity to the romance. The wild and raucous ways of the pirate life also lends itself to the use of various Bad Boy tropes such as the Rebel or the Rake.

In clean and inspirational romance, the Pirate is sometimes paired with the Reformed Bad Boy trope, with a hero who longs to leave his life of crime behind but who feels drawn back into it for complicated, though noble, reasons.

POTENTIAL WOUNDS

Misplaced loyalty
Being tortured
Being incarcerated for a crime
Failing to save someone's life
Being shipwrecked/stranded
Being forced to keep a dark secret
Serious injury or death of a crew member
Physical disfigurement
Being held captive
Crossing moral lines to survive

COMMON TRAITS

Fierce	Fearless	Charismatic
Passionate	Defiant	Adventurous
Daring	Commanding	Ruthless
Rebellious	Mysterious	Clever
Resourceful	Seafaring	Skilled fighter

WOODSMAN/LUMBERJACK

THIS TROPE FULFILLS THE READER'S DESIRE FOR A HERO WHO IS TRADITIONALLY MASCULINE AND DEEPLY ROOTED

The heart of any Woodsman romance is the compelling hero—a rugged and strong individual whose life is intertwined with the beauty and challenges of nature. His rough exterior and intimidating demeanor might be off-putting at first, but as the story unfolds, the draw of the love interest works its magic, melting even the hardest of hearts. The hero's transformation, as he gradually reveals his softer and more vulnerable side, becomes a powerful and heartwarming journey that captivates readers.

The majestic mountain or forest setting plays a pivotal role, adding an element of enchantment and allure to the narrative. The vast wilderness becomes a character in itself, mirroring the hero's independence, resilience, untamed beauty, and even serenity. Amid the breathtaking scenery, manual labor becomes an essential aspect of the Woodsman romance. Scenes of wood chopping, building fires, and other physical tasks not only add authenticity to the story but also highlight the hero's undeniable masculinity. His mastery of the wilderness and the skill with which he handles these tasks further solidifies his appeal as a captivating and competent protagonist.

While setting and manual labor set the stage, it is the character of the Woodsman that shines through as the heart of the story. His independence and self-sufficiency make him a compelling figure, drawing readers into his world and leaving them spellbound by his charisma and gruff charm.

WHY READERS LOVE IT

Readers are drawn to Woodsman/Lumberjack romance mainly for the rugged masculinity of the hero. His outdoorsy nature exudes strength, appealing to readers who appreciate characters that embody traditional notions of toughness and resilience. His competence in navigating the wilderness and handling manual labor tasks intensifies his allure, making him a captivating and capable protagonist.

Witnessing the transformation of the hero from a gruff and stoic figure to a vulnerable and loving partner is a deeply satisfying experience for readers. The power of love softens the hero's rough edges, exposing his emotional depth and making him a more relatable and endearing character. In this way, the Woodsman shares many characteristics with the other *Tough Guy* tropes.

Additionally, the setting of mountains or forests provides an escape from everyday life, transporting readers to a world of natural beauty and serenity. The lush landscapes and untamed wilderness add a sense of wonder and adventure to the romance, creating a captivating backdrop that enhances the emotional journey of the characters.

READER EXPECTATIONS

One of the most important aspects of the Woodsman/Lumberjack romance is the transformation of the hero as he falls in love. Readers expect to witness his emotional journey, as the love interest softens his rough exterior and reveals his vulnerability. The power of love is evident as the hero evolves from a gruff and intimidating figure to a tender and devoted partner. This is the central key to fulfilling the readers unspoken wish fulfillment for these stories.

However, the woodsman isn't the only character in these books. The natural beauty of the outdoors becomes a character of its own. The setting will naturally involve the wilderness, with picturesque scenes of mountains, forests, hunting lodges, or remote cabins. Small towns and forest ranger stations might also serve as charming backdrops, offering a sense of community and intimacy that complements the romance.

The romance should authentically portray the challenges and dangers of living and working in the woods. Lumberjack novels often culminate in gripping crises that involve injury on the job, encounters with wild animals, or other natural hazards. These thrilling moments add tension and excitement to the narrative, highlighting the hero's courage and resilience in the face of adversity.

COMMON PITFALLS

Toxic masculinity: As with other traditionally masculine heroes, you will want to steer clear of glorifying any of the more commonly criticized masculine traits of aggression, dominion/control or chauvinism.

Environmental responsibility: As already stated, these characters should have a deep and abiding love for nature, so be sure that this translates to responsible use of the land and forestry. This will help you to avoid the ire of readers who are passionate about issues like conservation and preservation of nature and deforestation.

Too dumb to live: Since our hero is in his element and extremely competent, it can be tempting to make our heroine his foil—completely useless and incompetent. But we don't like dumb characters. She may need to be rescued, she can be unfamiliar with the setting and the tasks at hand—but make sure she isn't too dumb to live.

COMMONLY PAIRED TROPES

The Woodsman is often a tough, strong character which, coupled with his physical location in the woods, lends itself to a Lone Wolf/Recluse internal trope. These characters are often paired as a protector for a Damsel in Distress or acting as some sort of Bodyguard.

Fish Out of Water is one of the most common pairings for this character, with another character suddenly forced to rely on the land like he is so skilled at doing. Another common pairing is the Amnesia trope, where a woman shows up under mysterious circumstances or sustained injury in a car accident near his home in the woods and he must play Caretaker.

POTENTIAL WOUNDS

Misplaced loyalty
Being let down by a trusted organization
Losing a spouse
Being rejected by peers
Being falsely accused of a crime
Not being able to protect someone they love

COMMON TRAITS

Strong	Self-reliant	Skilled
Capable	Resourceful	Pragmatic
Outdoorsy	Tough	Stoic
Nature loving	Resilient	Adventurous
Gruff	Hardworking	Grounded

VIKING

---

*THIS TROPE FEEDS THE READER'S
DESIRE FOR ADVENTURE AND A
FIERCELY LOYAL HERO*

Viking romances often take place in the rugged and adventurous world of the Viking Age, with epic landscapes, battles, and epic journeys. The backdrop of raids and exploration adds an adventurous dimension to the romance. Due to the overlapping of time periods, these novels are closely linked to Highlander (many of which are set in the Middle Ages) and Medieval romances.

A Viking romance revolves around a (usually male) warrior from the 8th to 11th century Scandinavian Viking culture; Norwegian Vikings are especially prominent. These novels blend historical elements with passionate love stories, exploring the challenges that arise from the clash of cultures, raids, and exploration. They feature seafaring heroes (and heroines) who may be warriors, explorers, or traders. The characters are almost always physically strong due to the rugged nature of life in the Viking culture.

Viking romances may be set on an ocean voyage or in a Viking settlement, or a combination of the two. Settings such as longships sailing across stormy seas add to the overall allure and excitement of the story. You may find the *Romance Writer's Encyclopedia Volume 4: Setting Tropes* to be a helpful resource when writing about sea voyage settings.

This trope is distinct because it includes very tough men AND women. The female characters tend to be strong-willed, independent and willing to go against societal norms. They are willing to defend themselves, their people, and their principles, even if it comes with great risks. The men typically have a reputation to be feared, especially as warriors, but as their protective nature is drawn out by the love interest, they are likely to reveal a more tender, gentle side.

WHY READERS LOVE IT

One of the greatest appeals of these stories is the way in which they transport readers to a world of longships, raids, and battles for supremacy among rival clans. The Viking Age is a fascinating and less-explored period in history, and readers enjoy experiencing it through the eyes of the characters. These stories have an almost epic feel that sweeps readers away to another time and place.

Viking heroes are strong, rugged, and daring, with a wild spirit. These larger-than-life heroes battle against all odds to find love, treasure, and a place in history. Readers admire their determination, courage, and willingness to sacrifice in order to preserve their way of life.

Just as in Pirate romances, the trope-defining protagonist in these stories may be a woman, and the women are no less fierce than the men. Heroines are typically strong and capable women who refuse to be limited by the expectations of their society. They may be shield-maidens, skilled fighters who defend their homes and families alongside their male counterparts. They may also be powerful chieftains, mystics, or healers, who use their intelligence and resourcefulness to lead their people to safety and prosperity.

Readers love to see these heroines demonstrate agency and autonomy in a world where women had limited freedoms, making it easy to root for the strong female characters who defy expectations.

One of the most common themes explored in these novels is the concept of loyalty and honor. While the Vikings are often stereotyped as ruthless raiders, in actuality, trust and loyalty were integral values in their society. Regardless of which social class your character belongs to, they would be expected to remain loyal to their leader, even in the face of great danger. This passionate and unwavering devotion is not only admirable, but it's downright swoon-worthy when extended to the heroine.

READER EXPECTATIONS

The biggest unspoken expectation of these stories is that the stories are equally about adventure or excitement and romance. These intense, action-packed scenes should be balanced with more intimate moments of romance and emotional connection, similar to the pacing of a romantic suspense.

Kidnappings and raids are common plot elements in Viking romance novels, as they capture the adventurous and tumultuous spirit of the Viking Age. These elements are often used to create tension, conflict, and passionate relationships between the characters. In many Viking romances, one of the central characters is either kidnapped or captured by the other. This creates an initial power dynamic where one character holds the other captive. The dynamics of captor and captive can lead to intense emotional interactions, as they are forced to confront their feelings and desires in the midst of adversity. Over the course of the story, the captor character may undergo a transformation, becoming more sympathetic or morally conflicted. This can lead to a redemption arc and a shift in the power dynamic within the relationship.

While not entirely ubiquitous in the trope, Alpha Males are a common archetype in these stories where the hero exudes confidence and commands respect. You might read the entry on Alpha Males for more information on the character arc of these Characters. The Viking hero's tough exterior often hides emotional wounds or a troubled past, but as the relationship progresses, the heroine's love and influence help him heal and transform into a better person.

It is also not unusual for these stories to have hints of mysticism, folklore, or magical elements. We cover this more in the settings volume of the *Romance Writer's Encyclopedia*, but due to the superstitious nature of the cultures, your characters are likely influenced by widespread polytheism and belief in omens or other superstitions.

Viking society was built on values such as honor, loyalty, and bravery. These themes often play a significant role in the characters' actions and decisions. Another theme often explored in Viking romance novels is the idea of duty. In these societies, duty to one's family, clan, or crew was of utmost importance, and individuals who shirked their duties were often punished harshly. Viking romance novels may depict characters who must carry out their duties as warriors or leaders, even in the face of danger or personal sacrifice.

COMMON PITFALLS

Glamorizing violence: Both Vikings and pirates are often associated with brutality and, while it would be unrealistic to completely shy away from this, your readers will have a difficult time connecting with and rooting for the happily ever after of a brutal and violent Viking warrior. Instead, focus on the hero's sense of justice and honor.

Non-consensual relationships: Consent is crucial in any romance story. Because the clan-dynamic of the Viking society often lends itself to stories of kidnapping and arranged marriage, authors should be cautious not to romanticize or normalize non-consensual relationships. Instead, focus on building relationships based on mutual respect, trust, and understanding between the hero and the heroine.

Superficial cultural representation: When portraying Vikings, avoid shallow and stereotypical depictions of their cultures. Conduct thorough research to accurately portray their customs, beliefs, and way of life. Vikings had a well-established and organized society, so be sure to respectfully incorporate these cultural elements to add depth and authenticity to the story, even as you add your own fictional world-building intricacies.

COMMONLY PAIRED TROPES

Like Pirate novels, Viking romances are most commonly paired with Damsel in Distress, giving the character an opportunity to show their kindness and compassion. Often, these heroes are prohibited from engaging with the heroine due to kidnapping or conflict with outside forces, creating a classic combination with the Forbidden Love or Enemies to Lovers tropes.

Many Viking romance novels involve situations where the hero and heroine are in Forced Proximity, often due to circumstances like kidnapping, raids, or arranged marriages. The use of these trope combinations is also often paired with Time Travel, which seems to highlight the common theme of clashing cultures by sending a contemporary love interest into Viking territory.

VIKING

Due to the prevalence of Norse mythology during the Viking Age, it is also common for these novels to be mixed with fantasy, in what many readers and authors call romantasy.

POTENTIAL WOUNDS

Misplaced loyalty
Being shunned
Living through social unrest
Failing to save someone's life
Being shipwrecked/stranded
Being kidnapped
Being forced to keep a dark secret
Bearing the responsibility for many deaths
A nomadic childhood

COMMON TRAITS

Mysterious	Defiant	Rebellious
Seafaring	Unyielding	Resourceful
Charismatic	Fierce	Fearless
Adventurous	Passionate	Intrepid
Ruthless	Daring	Commanding

CHAPTER 15

BACKSTORY AND EMOTIONAL BAGGAGE TROPES

THESE TROPES FULFILL THE READER'S DESIRE TO BE LOVED DESPITE THEIR PAST OR CIRCUMSTANCES.

It's never too late to find love.

For the *Backstory and Emotional Baggage* tropes, the process of opening up to love again is a central theme. Readers look for realistic portrayals of the emotional challenges and growth that accompany this journey.

These stories are relatable, engaging, and often total tearjerkers. The focus on backstory and emotional baggage makes these characters incredibly relatable and authentic to readers.

CHAPTER 15

At their core, each of these tropes is something of a second chance romance. A second chance at love for the widow(er) or the seasoned character. A second chance to have the family of their dreams for the single parent. These stories are full of healing and redemptive themes, and readers can't help but empathize deeply with the heroes and heroines of these novels when done well.

SEASONED CHARACTERS

SINGLE PARENT

WIDOW(ER)

SEASONED CHARACTERS

THIS TROPE FULFILLS THE READER'S DESIRE TO KNOW THAT IT IS NEVER TOO LATE TO FIND TRUE LOVE

The Seasoned Characters trope offers a refreshing and compelling departure from conventional romance narratives that typically feature younger protagonists. Within this genre, the focus shifts to heroes and heroines in their 50s, 60s, 70s, or even older, allowing readers to immerse themselves in stories of love and passion experienced by characters with a lifetime of wisdom and life experiences.

These seasoned romances delve into the complexities of mature relationships, where characters come with grown children, past marriages, and the emotional baggage that comes from a life well-lived. Instead of navigating the trials of early adulthood, these protagonists grapple with the challenges of second chances, finding love after loss, and rediscovering themselves within the context of new relationships.

WHY READERS LOVE IT

As Seasoned romance continues to gain popularity, its appeal lies in the authentic and relatable portrayal of characters who mirror the experiences of a growing demographic of romance readers. Many readers, well beyond their thirties, find solace in the relatability and wisdom of seasoned characters, finding reflections of their own lives and aspirations in the lives of the characters. The trope allows for a celebration of love, passion, and emotional growth that

217

transcends age, showing that romance and happiness are not exclusive to the younger generation, but can blossom at any stage of life.

Another reason readers love Seasoned romance is the depth and complexity it brings to the genre. These characters have lived long and eventful lives, encountering both joy and sorrow, success and failure. Their emotional baggage and life experiences add layers of richness to the narrative, making the journey toward love and happiness even more profound. The struggles faced by Seasoned Characters feel relatable and honest, evoking empathy and admiration from readers who have encountered similar hurdles in their own lives.

Furthermore, Seasoned romance challenges societal norms surrounding age and love. By showcasing vibrant and passionate love stories among mature characters, the genre defies ageist stereotypes and reiterates that romance knows no bounds. Readers are inspired by the idea that love can thrive at any stage of life, proving that it is never too late to find love, take chances, and embrace new beginnings. The emphasis on emotional growth, self-awareness, and the resilience of Seasoned Characters offers a message of hope and optimism.

READER EXPECTATIONS

In writing Seasoned Characters, readers expect authors to craft individuals with rich backstories and life experiences that have shaped their personalities and worldviews. These characters come with baggage and emotional wounds that go beyond the typical high school drama or early dating struggles. Instead, they may have faced life-altering events like divorces or the loss of a spouse, which have undoubtedly influenced their present circumstances and attitudes.

A significant aspect of Seasoned romances is the presence of grown children, grandkids, and complex family dynamics. Authors are tasked with depicting the complexities of blended families and the challenges that arise when two people with established lives and relationships come together. The interactions with adult children and the navigation of family bonds add depth and realism to the narrative.

Readers anticipate protagonists who exhibit self-awareness, maturity, and wisdom. Seasoned Characters have lived long enough to gain valuable life experience, leading to decisions and actions marked by a sense of pragmatism and emotional intelligence. As full-grown adults, they have likely learned from past mistakes and are less likely to tolerate miscommunication or deceit in relationships.

Moreover, these characters bring a unique perspective on starting over and taking chances on love later in life. Often these characters have been alone for quite a while, and starting over with someone new is terrifying and exciting at the same time. They've made their own decisions for years and adjusting to a new relationship is a challenge they will have to overcome.

COMMON PITFALLS:

Act your age: The most common complaint we see about authors venturing into this trope is that the characters don't act their age. Either the characters are written as geriatric when they are only in their early 60s or acting far too young, making impulsive decisions and avoiding simple conversations in their embarrassment. If you are writing in this trope and you are NOT in this age bracket, get a sensitivity reader. One who isn't afraid to call you out for making your 60-year-old character sound like an 85-year-old nursing home patient when they are, in fact, still walking four miles a day and chasing their grandchild three mornings a week.

Neglecting physical attraction: Physical attraction and intimacy are important components of any romance. Avoid the misconception that older characters aren't interested in or capable of experiencing this aspect of a relationship. You don't have to get graphic, but recognize that there is a physical aspect to relationship, regardless of age.

Overemphasizing age: While age is a factor, don't make it the sole defining trait of the characters. Focus on their personalities, dreams, and growth rather than constantly reminding readers of their age.

Assuming lack of adventure: Older characters are not limited to quiet, sedentary lives. They can still seek adventure, travel, and enjoy new experiences.

COMMONLY PAIRED TROPES

Seasoned Characters pair wonderfully with other relational tropes that bring additional complications—Second Chance romance, Friends to More, Workplace romances. They also pair nicely with several other character tropes like Cowboy, Billionaire, Widow(er). They are harder to pull off with tropes that rely on a bit of "immaturity" of the characters—Enemies to Lovers, Brother's Best Friend, and Fake Relationships to name a few.

POTENTIAL WOUNDS

Choosing to not be involved in the life of a child
Losing a child
Losing a spouse/significant other
Suffering from infidelity

Financial ruin due to a spouse's irresponsibility
Divorce or abandonment
Being fired or laid off

COMMON TRAITS

Wise	Empathetic	Charismatic
Reflective	Resilient	Insightful
Patient	Sincere	Caring
Accomplished	Adventurous	Dignified
Gracious	Serene	Tenacious

SINGLE PARENT

THIS TROPE FULFILLS THE READER'S DESIRE FOR STRONG MEN TO EMBRACE THE ROLE OF FATHERHOOD AND FOR LOVE TO PREVAIL DESPITE DIFFICULT CIRCUMSTANCES

Romances featuring single parents center around characters navigating the challenges of parenting while seeking a romantic connection. Whether they are widowed, divorced, or have never been married, these protagonists carry emotional baggage that must be confronted to embrace love once again. The children of the Single Parent play a vital role in the narrative, becoming an integral part of both the story and their parent's life.

The Single Parent can be the hero or heroine of the story, each with their unique struggles and vulnerabilities. Their journey involves balancing the demands of parenthood with the pursuit of a new relationship. These characters tend to be incredibly relatable, while exhibiting strength, resilience, and vulnerability. As readers witness their struggles and triumphs, they become emotionally invested in the characters' happiness.

The love interest may enter the Single Parent's life through chance encounters, shared interests, or mutual connections, and they will likely connect through shared values, interests, or experiences. In most of these stories, the Single Parent will have some difficulty juggling their responsibilities while making room for their own personal happiness and romantic pursuits. The journey of opening up to love can be fraught with doubts and hesitations; because of that, this trope is often paired with slow burn romances.

WHY READERS LOVE IT

Readers naturally feel empathy for characters who are doing their best to provide a good life for their children while overcoming their circumstances and navigating their own personal growth and relationships. It takes grit and resilience to parent on your own. There is a degree of maturity that comes along with parenthood, and while these characters may not have it all figured out, they are fighting tooth and nail to get there for the benefit of their family.

Readers are drawn to the realism of Single Parent romances, as they feature characters facing the everyday challenges of parenthood and navigating complex family situations. The portrayal of imperfect, broken individuals striving to find love despite their pasts resonates with readers on a personal level. This genuineness makes the characters easy to connect with, fostering empathy and a deeper emotional investment in their love story.

The presence of endearing children adds an element of heartwarming sweetness to the narrative. The bond between the single parent and their children tugs at the heartstrings, and readers find joy in witnessing the characters grow as a family. The single parent loves to watch her children fall for her love interest too. Moreover, the notion of found family, where love transcends blood ties, holds a strong appeal, making readers cherish the unbreakable bonds that form in these romances.

The idea of second chances at love resonates deeply with readers. The single parent's journey to open their heart and find healing after past heartbreaks is a powerful and transformative experience. These books are deliciously messy. For a parent who has become accustomed to putting the needs of their child before themselves (including their love life), the love interest's entrance into their life and heart has a tendency to get emotions and priorities all tangled up. These complications not only enhance the reader's connection to these characters, but it heightens the tension and keeps your readers turning the pages all the way to the happily ever after.

READER EXPECTATIONS

Readers expect to see strong family dynamics in Single Parent romances, with the parent-child relationship playing a significant role. The interactions and bond between the single parent and their children should be well-developed and central to the narrative, and the children should be well-developed characters in their own right.

The challenges and joys of parenthood should be realistically portrayed, depicting the responsibilities, routines, and emotional highs and lows of raising children. The kids have to play a role in the story, because they mean *everything* to your single parent character. It is worth addressing challenges that arise from blending two lives, such as introducing the child to the romantic interest or dealing with potential resistance from others. At some point during the second act, you should attempt to show how the child reacts to the new romantic interest and the changes in their family dynamics.

Most often, the "Shields Up" beat of the romance will have something to do with the children and the impact of the relationship on them—with the Single Parent character sacrificing their own desires for what they perceive to be the good of the child. Because the stakes of failure are so high, these relationships also tend toward slow burn pacing, with lots of tension and anticipation while the characters wrestle with their feelings and the reasons they shouldn't give in to them.

Secondary characters, such as friends and extended family, often contribute to the story's richness and offer support to the single parent and their children. These characters help to illustrate the challenges that single parents face, such as time constraints, financial pressure, and work-life balance, because even the most capable of single parents will likely feel like they just can't keep up with all the demands on their own. These characters may form a found family, adding depth to the narrative and creating a sense of community and warmth that readers look for.

COMMON PITFALLS

Disappearing child: In a single-parent household, the child or children will inevitably be the central focus of your protagonist's life. So don't let your hero or heroine completely forget about their child once the love interest comes along; the romance will become the forefront of your novel, but that doesn't mean that the children disappear. It may be a challenge to find time alone due to parenting schedules, and your single parent may worry how the blossoming relationship will affect family dynamics. They may daydream about how the love interest will fit in perfectly to their lives. Whatever the case, much of your main character's journey will be finding the balance between personal and family life, so don't let the kids fall to the wayside as they become more invested in their love life.

Perfect, precocious kids: While it may be tempting to depict children as adorable and exceptionally mature for their age, it is essential to strike a balance and present them as authentic characters with their own flaws and age-appropriate behaviors. Readers may find it unrealistic or off-putting if the children behave in ways that are not developmentally appropriate for their age. Ensuring that the kids' actions, dialogue, and emotional responses align with their age and stage of development will create a more genuine and relatable portrayal of family dynamics in the romance.

Falling for the kids, not the love interest: The love interest *absolutely* should bond with and come to love the children of your single parent, but they need to fall for more than the idea of a happy little family. They need to form a true emotional and lasting bond with the protagonist. Emphasize open and honest communication between characters, addressing any misunderstandings, doubts, or fears that arise.

COMMONLY PAIRED TROPES

The Single Parent trope is often paired with a Damsel in Distress (or a Dude in Distress) where the single parent is increasingly overwhelmed with the workload and/or financial responsibility of being the sole earner and provider for a household. This naturally lends itself to other pairings where the love interest can help and support the single parent, like *Money, Money* tropes, Marriage of Convenience, or characters with strong "provider" tendencies like Cowboy or Man in Uniform.

The Single Mom trope may be paired with Secret Baby in a Second Chance romance—often this is in a Coming Home story or Small Town setting.

For Single Dad characters, a relationship with the Nanny is probably the most commonly paired trope. This trope has a delicate tension between the wounds of the Single Parent, the forbidden nature of the relationship, and both characters caring deeply for the child on their own.

POTENTIAL WOUNDS

Failing to provide for your child
A toxic relationship
Abandonment
Being disowned or shunned
Getting a divorce
Loss of a loved one

COMMON TRAITS

Nurturing	Strong	Devoted
Sacrificing	Selfless	Protective
Resilient	Patient	Adaptive
Determined	Resourceful	Compassionate
Caring	Loving	Responsible

WIDOW(ER)

THIS TROPE FULFILLS THE READER'S DESIRE FOR LOVE TO OVERCOME LOSS

The Widow(er) trope is poignant and emotionally charged, exploring the complexities of love and loss. In these heart-wrenching tales, one or both of the main characters have experienced the profound pain of losing their spouse, and they are left to grapple with the aftermath of grief and heartache. The journey of a Widow or Widower moving forward from their devastating loss and discovering the possibility of love again forms the crux of these stories. This trope delves into the raw and vulnerable emotions of characters as they navigate the path from being unwilling to move on to opening their hearts to the prospect of a new beginning with someone else.

The exploration of grief and healing is central to Widow(er) romances, providing readers with an intimate and relatable glimpse into the process of saying goodbye to a loved one. These stories deeply resonate with readers as they delve into the emotional roller coaster of loss and the slow, often challenging, road to healing. These stories will require your character to stretch themselves as they fight to find hope and happiness amidst their heartache. It is a struggle that ultimately makes the happily ever after richly rewarding for both the lovers and the reader.

You can use similar concepts if a character had a significant other die, even if they weren't married, though some of the wounds and obstacles may be slightly different. Losing a future with someone before you've had a chance to experience it is traumatic, for sure. Losing the person you walked alongside through years and milestones is a different kind of loss.

This trope can be difficult to write. It requires a delicate growth arc, where the Widow or Widower moves from "unwilling to move on" to "ready to start a life with someone else." An author must approach that character arc carefully. These are often slow burn romances with a lot of inner angst. A Widow(er) is likely to wrestle with guilt or shame at the idea of moving on, as well as anxiety at the idea of "starting from scratch" with someone new. When done properly, these tales of love, second chances, and resilience are deeply satisfying and unforgettable.

WHY READERS LOVE IT

There is something deeply moving about watching someone who has had their heart torn out and their life shattered be restored to life and happiness. It's this emotional depth and authenticity that draws readers to Widow(er) romances.

These tales resonate with readers because they capture the universal experience of grief and the transformative power of love. Witnessing characters who have endured the devastating loss of a spouse find happiness again is both heartrending and heartwarming, and it creates a profound emotional connection with the readers. The characters' struggles with guilt, shame, and anxiety at the thought of moving on resonates with readers, and it is easy for readers to become deeply invested in the Widow(er)'s journey of healing and finding the courage to open their hearts to new possibilities.

The hope and resilience depicted in widow(er) romances offer a powerful message of optimism and renewal. These stories serve as a reminder that love can be a source of healing and that the human spirit is capable of overcoming even the most profound grief. The emotional arc of the characters reflects the complexity of real-life healing processes. As readers invest in the characters' emotional journeys, they also find solace and inspiration in their triumph over tragedy. The ultimate satisfaction comes from witnessing the protagonists' transformation, culminating in a gratifying happily ever after.

There is often a secondary or support character who acts as a source of encouragement and advice, and offers a different perspective to help the Widow(er) see beyond their grief to the future that still awaits them. Whether it's through humor, a listening ear, a helping hand, or a shoulder for crying on, readers love these characters who offer some much-needed companionship without any romantic strings attached. Though this character is sometimes combined with the love interest, it is important that their role as supporter stands out prominently over their romantic interest in the Widow(er), otherwise their support may not feel genuine to the reader.

READER EXPECTATIONS

When delving into a Widow(er) romance, readers anticipate an emotional journey that navigates grief alongside the characters, but they also want a glimpse of the character's life before their loss, including life with the deceased spouse or partner. This contrast between their life before and after will highlight how deeply this loss effects their daily life and emotional state. As the romantic relationship develops, it's important to explore how memories of the deceased spouse impact the new relationship.

Readers expect the melancholic journey from "stuck on the past" to "ready for a new future" to be full of ups and downs, emotional angst, and convoluted emotions. The path through grief and mourning is not a straight-line journey, and readers want to be along for the ride.

The Widow(er) character is often depicted as initially closed off to the idea of loving again, perhaps adopting a Lone Wolf persona as their grief isolates them. Alternatively, they may find solace in friendships and hobbies, not considering the possibility of remarrying. The romance evolves as the love interest becomes a sensitive and supportive presence in the Widow(er)'s life, offering a connection that helps them come to terms with their loss. However, the love interest should not be pushy or uncaring, and the healing process should happen organically, without forcing the character to move on before they are ready.

The character arcs in Widow(er) romances involve healing from grief, and readers expect the romance to be a catalyst for this healing journey. The love interest provides a gentle challenge to the Widow(er)'s reluctance to move on, showing patience and understanding as they support the character through their emotional turmoil. Portray the grieving process realistically, acknowledging the stages of grief and the individual ways characters cope, allowing for both setbacks and moments of growth.

With all that emotional weight, it can be a challenge, but the process of falling in love anew should be depicted with all the excitement and joy of a fresh romance, even if the character has experienced love before. The author must reawaken the sense of "new love energy" within the character, while offering some sense of closure *without* erasing the memory of the deceased spouse. This is an incredibly delicate balance though—the reader doesn't want to wallow in grief without the joy and excitement of the new romance, so be sure to deliver that well.

COMMON PITFALLS

Awful previous relationship: Avoid writing their previous relationship as broken, abusive, or loveless. This certainly makes it easier to sell that the character has true "forever" feelings for the new character, but it can shortcut the growth of truly moving past the old relationship and leave the previous relationship feeling like a plot device. If the previous relationship was a difficult one, there should be wounds that stem from that and make the character reluctant to try again.

Perfect previous relationship: On the flip side, making the first marriage too perfect or dwelling too much on "the other woman" can make it difficult for your character (and your readers) to move on and truly show interest in their new love. And while it's important to show the contrast of the Widow(er)'s life before and after they've been struck by grief, you should be cautious not to spend an excessive amount of time on the nature of their relationship with the deceased spouse. Readers who become emotionally invested in the character's original love story might find it difficult to accept a new romance, feeling that it diminishes the significance of the past relationship.

Passively falling in love: Be sensitive enough to give your character's emotional journey the proper weight. Even if it has been several years since the death of a spouse, the difficulties of finding love again should not be glossed over. In addition, if the transition from grief to a new romance is handled insensitively or too quickly, readers might perceive it as trivializing the grieving process.

233

COMMONLY PAIRED TROPES

Widow(er)s are often paired with the other Emotional Baggage tropes of either Single Parent or Seasoned Character. However, they can also be powerful with tropes like Law Enforcement, Billionaire, or Lone Wolf.

As far as tropes in other framework categories, the Widow(er) is frequently paired with Grumpy/Sunshine, Boss/Employee, including Nanny or Maid, and Second Chance romance (for example, reuniting with a high school sweetheart after losing their spouse).

POTENTIAL WOUNDS

The death of a spouse
Financial ruin due to a spouse's irresponsibility
Infidelity
Losing a loved one due to a random act of violence
Losing a loved one to prolonged disease
Natural or man-made disaster
A loved one's suicide
Failing to protect someone

COMMON TRAITS

Grieving	Sensitive	Thoughtful
Resilient	Strong	Empathetic
Solitary	Independent	Graceful
Reflective	Compassionate	Mysterious
Stoic	Mature	Nostalgic

CHAPTER 16

PASSION AND COMPETENCE TROPES

THESE TROPES FULFILL THE READER'S DESIRE TO SEE PASSION, COMPETENCE, DISCIPLINE, AND STRENGTH IN THEIR PARTNER

The characters who make up the *Passion and Competence* trope aren't crazy geniuses who know everything about everything, they're experts in a single field. And yet, their potential for success in that field will seem nearly limitless due their confidence and tenacity.

These characters are not only exceptionally skilled, capable and confident at their respective endeavors—they possess an unwavering sense of purpose. Even as they encounter problems in their work and life, they utilize their skill, competence, and drive to see the problem through to a solution.

ATHLETE

COWBOY

COUNSELOR/PASTOR

DOCTOR/MEDICAL PROFESSIONAL

GENIUS/NERD/BOOKWORM

POLITICIAN

ATHLETE (AKA SPORTS ROMANCE)

THIS TROPE FEEDS INTO THE READER'S DESIRE TO SEE TOUGHNESS AND DRIVEN COMPETITIVENESS IN THEIR PARTNER

These stories feature protagonists who are Athletes, Coaches, or individuals connected to the sports industry. The setting often includes stadiums, training facilities, and the adrenaline-fueled atmosphere of competitive sports.

In sports romance, the characters' passion for their sport mirrors their emotional journey in love. These Athletes are intensely dedicated and determined, striving for excellence on and off the field. Whether it's basketball, football, soccer, or any other sport, the backdrop of competitive athletics adds an exciting layer of action and drama to the romantic narrative.

Don't limit yourself to only the most talked about sports. There are avid fans of all types of sports. Each sport will have its own team dynamics, rules, jargon, demographics and culture. You may hit the goldmine of an underserved market, but don't assume that you won't pull in other sports fans as well.

Behind the tough exteriors of Athletes lie insecurities, past traumas, and personal struggles. Their personal or relational struggles will affect their performance, whether negatively or positively, and in many ways, their success or failure on the field mirrors the trajectory of their personal and romantic life.

When writing a Professional Athlete, this trope will rely to some degree on the "rich and famous" aspect, like many of the *Money, Money* tropes. However, that isn't to say that a down-on-his-luck minor league player or haggard high school coach couldn't fall into the Athlete trope.

Remember, athletics started thousands of years ago as a training ground and stand-in for battles. They are strong, confident, and (often) successful—at least on the playing field. Love will be another story, at least at the start of *your* story. These heroes and heroines are competitive, and as professionals, they are known for being one of the best at what they do. They may be stubborn, tenacious, or confident. They will likely be dedicated and incredibly disciplined. Despite these strengths, don't forget to give them a hole to fill. Because of these attributes, athletes will have a unique approach to dealing with issues both on and off the field (or court).

WHY READERS LOVE IT

The readers who gravitate toward Sports Romance, or romance with an Athlete character trope, are likely to have some sort of athletic background themselves. It might have been growing up around sports or participating as a student-athlete. They might belong to a family of intense fans or be married to someone who watches football on the weekends. Fans watch sports to be entertained, so make these stories fun! Don't neglect the entertainment value of your story or your sports scenes, and don't be afraid to have a little fun with your characters in their personality and interactions.

In addition, these readers *love* competition. The competitive nature of sports lends itself to rivalries and tension, but they also push the Athlete to reach their highest potential and leave no effort unspent. These traits can make for charismatic and intriguing characters who aren't afraid to pursue what they want. The hard work, dedication, and discipline required to excel in sports are qualities that readers admire.

Finally, athletic heroes are portrayed as physically fit, strong, and skilled in their respective sports. Readers (and the love interest) are drawn to characters who excel in their field and can showcase impressive feats of athleticism.

READER EXPECTATIONS

Readers want to be taken "behind the scenes" in these stories. For Professional Athletes, interactions with fans can rarely be avoided. Their fan base affects their livelihood; it affects their popularity, and it may even affect their contracts. These interactions may vary (think crazed/obsessive fans, down to earth or opportunistic fans), but they are likely to play some role in your narrative.

When you're talking about behind the scenes, it also means making sure they get to know the entire person that shows up on the field. Readers want a fully fleshed out Athlete, not just a caricature. Consider factors such as where they are in their athletic career—are they satisfied? Have they accomplished what they hoped to?

It is unlikely that your athlete has been a loner their entire careers, even if they are somewhat reclusive now. In order to reach the pinnacle of their sport, they would need a solid group of supporters helping them to "make it," whether it's family, their community, or a coach, etc. Don't forget to use the supporting cast of your story to reveal additional depth to your character.

Which means, we don't want to miss out on the locker room! We don't mean for you to write scene after scene or paragraph after paragraph of carnal descriptions and crude jokes. *Please don't do that.* But you will be leaving out a huge chunk of interactions in your athlete's life if you neglect to show the camaraderie, team dynamics, and community of a sports team that takes place in the locker room.

Another aspect of sports that should not be neglected is the physical impact on the body. It's likely that injuries will be a part of your story, or that the threat of injury will have influence on the Athlete's choices and career. Given the constant threat of injury, Athletes are acutely aware that their career could be over in the blink of an eye. For many, that contributes to the way they conduct themselves— whether that manifests as diligent training, altering their play as they get older or suffer minor injuries, and for some, they may simply choose to enjoy themselves to the max for as long as it lasts.

In some ways, the Athlete has elements of a setting trope. Whatever the sport is, your athlete exists within that world and subculture. Make sure your reader experiences it too.

COMMON PITFALLS

Know what you write: Would you be surprised at this point if we told you that research is essential to getting this trope right? Because the sport your character participates in will be a focal point of your story, you need to be sure that you understand it. What are the rules, the jargon, the positions; know the particulars of the playing season and offseason, the typical routine for professionals or amateur players; how are players or teams likely to attempt something underhanded, what makes a player stand out in their respective sport?

Most Sports Romance readers will know right away if you don't know the sport you're writing about, so don't make the mistake of passing off guesses or assumptions as facts. If you choose to create a fictitious sports league, there may be more wiggle room, but readers may be thrown off if the rules and routines are incredibly different from real-world leagues. This isn't to say you need to be a die-hard fan of the sport in order to write about it, but you should know enough that you can pass yourself off as a fan.

Inaccurate representation of sports culture: Think about demographics—each country will have its own fan base for the most popular sports, and within the US, the fan base of sports is often influenced by demographics. For example, while football has the widest fan base among Americans, southern Americans are more likely to be college football fans than those in the northeast; baseball is more popular among affluent Americans and those with high school diplomas or lower are more likely to be fans of auto racing. The fan base of your sport will influence the culture and it will most likely be a part of your story.

Jargon jungle: Don't over explain the details of the sport or be overly technical—although you may feel like an expert on them, you don't need to make your reader an expert. On the other side, don't assume that your reader knows everything about the sport you are writing about. A smart guideline to follow is to use as much technical jargon as you need to make the story authentic and enough exposition to avoid confusing your reader. Use common terms whenever possible—bat, puck, ball, home run, strike out, slap shot, dribble, dunk. There are times when you must use a less familiar term—when that happens, explain to the reader what it is and why it's important to use the correct word.

Legal implications: Don't use the names of real people/teams. These are players and organizations whose success is largely dependent on their public image, and they can notice very quickly when their name shows up somewhere. In addition, the names and acronyms of professional sports leagues and teams in the US are trademarked; this means it is illegal to use these names for profit (like selling a book.) To avoid legal issues, keep any mention of real people to the periphery and avoid making disparaging remarks.

COMMONLY PAIRED TROPES

Because the Athlete is so flexible, they can be paired with tons of other relational and situational tropes. Opposites Attract, Homecoming, Caretaker (such as with an injured player), Fake Relationship, or a Marriage of Convenience could all serve for a good internal or external conflict for your athlete to shine.

You may also choose another character trope for your Athlete. If they are uber successful, take a look at the Celebrity trope. Perhaps they are a Bad Boy or a Single Parent as well as an Athlete. A competitive rodeo cowboy would be a fun cross between an Athlete and Cowboy trope.

POTENTIAL WOUNDS

A learning disability
Cracking under pressure
Making a very public mistake
Being the victim of a vicious rumor
Having parents who loved conditionally

Being raised by a narcissist
Growing up in the spotlight

COMMON TRAITS

Competitive	Persistent	Energetic
Confident	Focused	Ambitious
Loyal	Tenacious	Determined
Hardworking	Disciplined	Charismatic
Driven	Resilient	Adaptable

COWBOY

*THIS TROPE FULFILLS THE READER'S
DESIRE FOR HEROES WHO ARE
HARDWORKING AND ROOTED IN
FAMILY AND TRADITIONAL VALUES*

Whether set in contemporary times or in historical settings, these captivating stories feature heroes who embody the spirit of the Cowboy. Cowboys come in various flavors, from ranchers tending to vast landscapes, lawmen upholding justice, rodeo riders showcasing their daredevil skills to lone-wolf characters living off-the-grid, forging their own path.

The Cowboy romance holds deep-rooted connection with nature and their passion extends to a commitment to protect their land, family, and way of life. These heroes can be rough around the edges, daring, rebellious, humble, or compassionate, and it is their love for the land and the animals that sustain them.

From slow-paced small towns to vast open spaces, the western setting becomes an integral part of the Cowboy's story, providing a backdrop for his adventurous and sometimes tumultuous journey into love and self-discovery. Cowboy romances offer readers an opportunity to immerse themselves in a world where tradition, loyalty, and the untamed spirit of the Wild West converge to create a captivating and emotionally rich reading experience. While Cowboy romances can go hand in hand with the Small Town's slow pace and the know-your-neighbor lifestyle, oftentimes, these characters are also resistant to change, and they don't necessarily take kindly to new faces.

WHY READERS LOVE IT

At the core of Cowboy romance lies the celebration of deep-rooted traditions and values. Readers are drawn to heroes who honor their upbringing and prioritize loyalty, family, and heritage. The allure of the Cowboy lies in the charm of country living, evoking a sense of rugged chivalry that captivates readers' hearts. Cowboys embody hard work, resilience, and a "never back down" attitude, appealing to readers who appreciate characters thriving in the face of challenges.

Physical attributes play a significant role in the appeal of Cowboy romance. Muscular hands, tanned skin, and a strong physique acquired through the laborious tasks of farming and ranching add to the hero's allure.

While physical attributes are important, readers also swoon over the cowboy's manners and respect, which often stem from their close-knit family dynamics and brotherly camaraderie. The setting of ranch life becomes an essential element that readers fall in love with, making world-building and detailed setting descriptions crucial to create an immersive reading experience.

For readers, a Cowboy romance novel has all the appeal of the country life, without the dirt and the flies—so be sure to hone in on those aspects of country living and chivalry that will really make your readers swoon over your down-home hero. Have your characters spend some time in nature, working with animals, or helping family and friends.

READER EXPECTATIONS

Your readers will expect the Cowboy to work hard and do it with heart, seemingly thriving in the face of obstacles. While Cowboy romances offer a glimpse into a picturesque way of life, readers also expect the heroes to face challenges. These might range from financial hardships and threats to the ranch's livelihood to personal struggles and emotional obstacles. Overcoming these challenges adds depth to the characters and creates opportunities for growth and self-discovery.

Your cowboy may or may not speak with a drawl or ride a horse, but we can expect him to mind his manners and his mama. Readers expect the hero to demonstrate gentlemanly behavior, drawing on traditional values that honor family ties and a code of ethics. This sense of respect extends to their interactions with others, including fellow ranchers and members of the community.

You can expect that the physical labor involved with farming will result in rough and calloused hands, tanned skin and, of course, muscles. But don't just focus on arm muscles and abs . . . and never underestimate the appeal of a man's well-muscled legs and glutes in a pair of Carhartt pants. Don't forget the hat either. Whether it's on the cover or simply in the story, the Cowboy might reveal more than he intends with a tip of his hat or a toss onto the counter.

Family dynamics reign supreme in Cowboy stories, and even if your cowboy isn't part of a huge family of brothers running a ranch, he's part of a team, and that brotherhood is fun to read. Readers expect a fairly large cast of characters and will binge-read through long series located on the same ranch. Because readers fall in love with the setting of these romances almost as much as they fall for the heroes, you'll need to spend some time in your world building and setting description if your story is set on a ranch, but that will be covered more heavily in the fourth volume of the *Romance Writer's Encyclopedia*.

BREAKDOWN OF ARCHETYPES

Rodeo cowboy—Brazen, may be rebellious or have something of a Bad Boy aspect to him, but will also be persistent with a "dust yourself off and try again" attitude. He'll have a lot in common with the Athlete character.

Lone wolf or off-the-grid cowboy—May be jaded/cynical or socially awkward, principled, emotionally as well as physically guarded, often as a result of a past hurt; see more under Lone Wolf.

Law enforcement cowboy—Motivated by justice/good deeds, daring and willing to take risks, driven by instinct; see more under Men (and Women) in Uniform.

COMMON PITFALLS

What's under the hat: Make sure there's a cowboy under that Stetson—while we fully expect a few tips of the hat, be sure that your cowboy is made of meatier stuff than his boots, a plaid shirt, and a cowboy hat. He needs to be more than a Cowboy in name, so go deeper.

Know what you write: If you'll be incorporating animals or ranch life into your book, do a bit of research. There's plenty of variation (and surprises) in farming and ranching, but if your cowboy is out helping a cow birth in the middle of a snowstorm, be prepared to explain yourself because most cowboys are not breeding their heifers to birth in January.

COMMONLY PAIRED TROPES

Cowboys are such a huge character-driven market that they are commonly paired with almost every trope under the sun. Whether it also happens to be another character trope tie-in such as the archetypes we mentioned above, or another such as Single Parent or Bodyguard, these characters take on so many different dimensions.

Because family relationships are emphasized in these genres, tropes that challenge family ties with boundaries being crossed or dishonesty are popular due to the internal conflict they create in the character. Examples include Brother's Best Friend, Fake Relationship, and Marriage of Convenience.

POTENTIAL WOUNDS

Cracking under pressure
Failing to save someone's life
Experiencing the death of a parent
Living with an abusive caregiver
Not being a priority growing up
A life-threatening accident
A loved one's suicide

COMMON TRAITS

Rugged	Humble	Self-reliant
Hardworking	Determined	Tough
Loyal	Protective	Rowdy
Respectful	Adventurous	Confident
Courageous	Traditional	Honest
Independent	Chivalrous	Trustworthy

COUNSELOR/PASTOR

THIS TROPE FEEDS INTO THE READER'S DESIRE TO BE UNDERSTOOD BY THEIR PARTNER AT THE HEART LEVEL

The Counselor character trope refers to a character who provides emotional support, advice, and guidance to others, possibly even the love interest. Counselors are wise, experienced individuals who help others develop skills, overcome challenges, and achieve their goals. In inspirational romance, this role is often filled by the pastor hero or some other clergy position.

These characters tend to carry a heavy emotional burden due to the pressure of constantly serving as a source of strength and support for others. Their wisdom often comes from their own lived experience and trauma, but it is important to note that they have a genuine desire to help others, even when it requires significant sacrifices to their own desires, goals, or needs.

They may impart knowledge and offer lessons through direct instruction or by allowing the protagonist to learn from their own actions. They can also act as protectors, shielding other characters from harm and providing a safe space for them to learn and grow.

At the archetypal level, the central role of the counselor is to facilitate the protagonist's personal growth and transformation. In a romance novel, this often means that the Counselor will have a pivotal role and influence in the transformation arc of the love interest, although sometimes it is not the love interest but someone they deeply care about. Seeing the impact of the Counselor on their loved ones, in this case, draws the love interest in as they grow to appreciate the tenderness and nurturing spirit of the Counselor.

While the Counselor/Pastor is admirable and respected by many, they are by no means perfect. Their own flaws will become increasingly evident to themselves and others as they are faced with the conflict and pursuit of true love.

The Counselor's character arc is often played out as they counsel a third party through a similar situation, forcing themselves to look at the disconnect between their own advice and their actions. They may encourage others to forgive while they hold on to bitterness, but their self-awareness in the face of this mirror leads to their transformation and growth.

WHY READERS LOVE IT

Readers are drawn to Counselor characters in romance novels because they offer a unique blend of qualities that can be both intriguing and heartwarming. These individuals tend to possess strong moral compasses and unwavering integrity, and this virtuous nature appeals to readers seeking characters with a sense of honor and principles.

Stories with a Counselor hero or heroine often engage with themes of healing and redemption, which resonate with readers who enjoy stories of personal transformation and second chances. In many cases, the Counselor must overcome their own personal struggles or past mistakes before embracing love, leading to powerful and satisfying character growth.

Christian readers love Pastor romances because it sets them up to be an exemplary leader of the home, as clergy are charged to be men above reproach. In addition to this, readers love the humanization paired with the spiritual depth of these characters. Finally, there is almost nothing as tantalizing as the inherent contrast between a Pastor hero's spiritual role and the challenges of a romantic relationship, setting the stage for depth, conflict, and a compelling narrative arc.

READER EXPECTATIONS

These characters are expected to possess emotional intelligence and empathy. Readers look for characters who can understand and connect with the emotions of other characters, which ultimately creates an intensely strong bond between the love interests.

Because of this emotional skill and the expectation of skillful communication, readers will become frustrated if conflicts between love interests are the result of miscommunication or misunderstanding. Readers expect the Counselor to be able to engage in meaningful and open conversations with the love interest (even if they are not especially willing, the Counselor should be skilled at drawing these things out). Furthermore, given their problem-solving abilities, readers will appreciate seeing how the hero urges their love interest to overcome relational challenges.

Authors should highlight the caring and supportive nature of these characters. Readers will expect the hero to be there for the heroine (or any other character) during her moments of vulnerability, offering space for her to open up and share her feelings, fears and doubts.

COUNSELOR/PASTOR

While the Counselor may be compassionate and nurturing, he should also possess inner strength and resilience. This balance creates a character who can be both a source of support and a protector. It is also this resilience that makes it compelling for readers to experience the Counselor sort through his own internal or relational struggles. Their heightened awareness and self-reflection allows these characters to deeply engage their inner conflict and find their well-earned happily ever after.

COMMON PITFALLS

Too preachy: The moral character of these heroes easily lends itself to falling into the sermon trap. While it may not occur as an actual church sermon (although . . . it often does), it may also be any type of lecture or extended monologue by the mentor/teacher/pastor character that comes at the most convenient moment of another character's transformation arc. Readers tend to gloss over these scenes at best, and at worst they may wholly disengage with the character.

Offering unsolicited advice: This person will obviously be a source of support and advice for many, but be sure that you do not portray them as a busybody who inserts themselves and their righteousness into every situation. Everyone can relate to receiving unsolicited advice, and it's one of the easiest ways to turn readers off of your character.

Imbalance of power/influence: The Counselor holds a position of influence, which can raise concerns about consent and exploitation especially when paired with the Age Gap trope. Ensure that the love interest has agency and makes their own decisions rather than being coerced or manipulated by the Counselor's position of influence.

COMMONLY PAIRED TROPES

Counselor/Pastor characters are often paired with other tropes that give them a rich backstory of personal growth or trials before the story begins. Reformed Bad boy, Widower, or Seasoned Characters are examples of such tropes.

Additionally, these characters are often paired with tropes that force internal conflict of the characters, such as tropes that play on dishonesty (Forbidden Romance, Marriage of Convenience, Fake Relationship, or Hidden Identity). Giving your Counselor/Pastor a strong motive to engage in deceit that is counter to their natural integrity is crucial to making these pairings work.

Other tropes that allow the Counselor to showcase their helping and compassionate nature are also popular. These include Single Parent, Damsel in Distress, Runaway Bride, Protector, and Fish Out of Water.

POTENTIAL WOUNDS

Leading someone astray in the past
Being forced to keep a dark secret
Being let down by a trusted organization
Being disappointed by a role model
Failing to do the right thing
Battling a mental disorder
Becoming a caregiver at a young age
Being falsely accused of a crime

COMMON TRAITS

Caring	Hopeful	Humble
Compassionate	Encouraging	Authentic
Altruistic	Supportive	Wise
Empathetic	Articulate	Open
High EQ	Personable	Patient
Optimistic	Understanding	Self-aware

DOCTOR/MEDICAL PROFESSIONAL

THIS TROPE FULFILLS THE READER'S DESIRE FOR A HERO WHO IS A CARETAKER

The Medical Professional romance trope offers a vast array of possibilities as it delves into the lives of protagonists working in the dynamic and demanding medical field. From doctors and nurses to specialists and paramedics, the options for medical professionals are endless. This trope allows authors to explore various medical disciplines, time periods, and locales, providing a fresh take on a beloved theme.

In these romances, at least one, if not both, protagonists work in the medical field, creating opportunities for compelling and emotionally charged storylines. The romance may blossom between a medical professional and their patient or a family member of the patient. Moreover, authors can choose to focus on characters during their education or training, such as nursing school, medical school, residency, or fellowship.

The characters in medical professional romances are often perceived as aloof, distant, or too preoccupied with work to fall in love. As the romance evolves, the story should showcase the characters' growth, demonstrating how they prioritize their relationship and navigate the delicate balance between work and love.

DOCTOR/MEDICAL PROFESSIONAL

Professionals who may be depicted in a medical romance include:

- Doctors
    - General practice
    - Hospitalists
- Surgeons
- Nurses
- EMT and Paramedic (*please* take time to understand the difference between these two)
- Specialists
    - Cardiologist
    - Endocrinologist
    - Oncologist
    - Neurologist
- Occupational therapist
- Physical therapist
- Medical or surgical technician

WHY READERS LOVE IT

One of the primary reasons readers are drawn to Medical Professional romances is the high-pressure environment and the life-and-death situations the characters face. The medical field presents ample opportunities for tension and conflict, making the stories emotionally charged and intense. With lives hanging in the balance, the characters must deal with high-stakes situations, medical emergencies, ethical dilemmas, and serious illnesses. This intensity translates well to the romance, as the characters grapple with complex emotions like grief, loss, and trauma, creating a powerful exploration of the human experience.

As much as we know that people go into the medical field for a huge variety of reasons, we still want to believe that their goal is to help people. We want to trust and respect our medical personnel, and that's why they make good heroes and heroines for romances. They bring with them an inherent level of likeability, just by being someone who helps people who are hurting. Readers are naturally inclined to admire and respect medical personnel due to their roles as caregivers and healers. Now, that's not to say some Doctors aren't jerks. We've all seen *House, MD*, right? But if your main character is detached and emotionless while caring for patients, we better understand why.

READER EXPECTATIONS

When diving into a Medical Professional romance, readers expect to witness the impact of the characters' medical careers on their thoughts and narrative. When someone coughs, do they think about the virus they've seen in their office or the prediction that this flu season is going to be particularly rough? Do they think about the patient who recently died after a long battle with pneumonia?

Readers want to see the Medical Professionals' knowledge and experiences influencing their perspectives, making the story authentic and immersive. The inclusion of medical details and injuries should be well-researched and thoughtfully integrated into the narrative, enhancing the credibility of the story.

Research is going to be key in this trope as well. If you don't have medical training yourself, be sure to get your hands on some excellent resources and reach out to friends who are nurses or doctors. They'll be glad to answer simple questions. There are also some guides to medicine written specifically for authors that can help with setting, characters, and injuries.

COMMON PITFALLS

Relying on Doctor McHottie: Your lovers will obviously find one another pleasing to the eye, but don't diminish your doctor (or any other professional for that matter) down to eye-candy. Your characters are highly skilled and hardworking; they have learned through years of dedication and surely made some mistakes. If their only personality trait is being good at everything and looking good while doing it, you have failed to develop any depth of character to engage and entice the reader.

Inaccurate healthcare processes: While the process and procedure will vary between facilities, insurance systems and location, you should seek some basic understanding of how long test results would take, what types of doctors would be needed for various conditions, as well as what a realistic treatment plan would look like. These details will go a long way in making the experience more authentic to the reader.

Inaccurate medicine/physiology: Again, do your research. An X-ray won't show you if there is an infection. Lab work won't show you if there is swelling in the brain. Know what you need and then use the correct medical procedures to get you there, and don't use terms willy-nilly.

Token sick people: Avoid having sick/injured characters who are only there to make the hero or heroine look good.

Too much jargon/detail: Especially if you have medical training, don't forget that many of your readers will not. If you're using abbreviations, scientific names, or jargon, make sure it is sparse and well-explained. And don't get too gross—readers aren't here for anything that oozes. Technical scenes may feel like a great place to show off your medical knowledge and tap into your skills of describing wounds and gore, but remember the genre. The open-heart surgery your character performs in the second act may be a critical moment for character development, but focus on the character's emotional journey in that scene rather than the chest cracked wide open in front of her.

Not including support staff: Hospitals and clinics are largely populated by people who are not doctors. These include nurses, therapists (respiratory, occupational, physical), physicians assistants, nurse practitioners, medical assistants, dieticians, social workers, technicians, transport, custodians, clerks . . . Seriously, the list goes on. Don't make every side character in your book a fellow doctor.

COMMONLY PAIRED TROPES

Medical Professionals are often paired with other characters that they would encounter in Workplace romances, including Law Enforcement, Firefighters/EMTs and other Medical Professionals. Other characters that they might encounter as patients or patients' family (such as a Single Parent or Counselor) are also popular pairings.

The other commonly paired tropes often revolve around placing a driven medical professional in a situation that either pulls them away from their career and unbalances their priorities (such as Instant Family or Vacation romances) or tropes that allow the Doctor to showcase their skills in a non-typical location such as Stranded or On the Run.

POTENTIAL WOUNDS

Failing to save someone's life
Cracking under pressure
Battling a mental disorder
Accidentally killing someone
Being unfairly blamed for someone's death
Being disappointed by a role model
Being raised by parents who loved conditionally

COMMON TRAITS

Altruistic	Skilled	Dedicated
Committed	Compassionate	Resilient
Passionate	Ethical	Knowledgeable
Driven	Empathetic	Healing
Intelligent	Caring	Diligent

GENIUS/NERD/BOOKWORM

THIS TROPE FEEDS THE READER'S DESIRE TO BE ACCEPTED AS THEY ARE, FOR THEIR BRAIN AS WELL AS THEIR BEAUTY

At its core, this trope revolves around heroes and heroines distinguished by their exceptional intellect and unwavering passion for academic pursuits. These characters often possess a unique charm that sets them apart, capturing readers' hearts with their unassuming brilliance. Their journey unfolds as they navigate the complexities of relationships, self-discovery, and personal growth in the midst of academic fervor.

These characters may wear their passion as a badge of honor, dedicating themselves to pursuits that ignite their souls. However, this intensity can occasionally manifest as social awkwardness, leading to feelings of being out of place or seen as outsiders in conventional social settings.

The unique perspective of the Genius or Nerd often casts them as underdogs or outcasts, overlooked by potential love interests and underestimated by adversaries. It is important to provide ample opportunities for their innate talents to shine. For characters who begin the tale as misfits, their evolution involves a journey of self-acceptance and the realization that their natural strengths are their greatest assets, fostering newfound confidence.

WHY READERS LOVE IT

Writing a bookish heroine who dreams of being Belle—free to roam the Beast's library—is a surefire way to connect with your readers. Same goes for writing a hero who isn't afraid to show his passion about the latest tech gadget he invented. Or maybe he forgets that not everyone cares whether the efficiency of lithium batteries can be increased incrementally if we just tweak that one thing, as he runs his fingers through his mussed hair and jots down a few more notes . . . Phew, is it hot in here? The passion and intelligence of these characters really resonates with readers who appreciate the pursuit of knowledge and the charm of intellectual conversations.

But romance readers are also firm believers that being the smartest person in the room doesn't mean a thing if you always end up in that room alone at the end of the night. They want to see these quirky characters find their perfect match. Someone who sees and appreciates them for the intelligent, unique, wonderful person they are. Simply put, being passionate about something (especially something intellectual) makes for an interesting, engaging character. These characters are the opposite of apathetic, and that invites readers into their particular flavor of excitement.

Readers love the quirky charm and relatability of these heroes and heroines, so lean into it! Don't be afraid to highlight any quirks or eccentricity that makes them stand out and endears the love interest and the reader to them! When it comes to the underestimated hero, readers love to see the underdog rise to victory. Connect with the reader's empathy and give your hero plenty of opportunity to overcome obstacles and succeed against all odds. It is this journey of self-discovery that resonates with readers' desire for authenticity, growth, and the ability to find love while remaining true to oneself.

READER EXPECTATIONS

Readers expect intelligent heroes AND heroines, no matter which one is intended as the Genius or Geek of the story. The genius-level IQ hero isn't going to remain interested in a shallow Malibu Barbie character. Her intelligence and depth may be hidden, but it needs to be there to keep him intrigued—even better if the other main character is a bit of a puzzle your protagonist needs to solve. *Understanding* is a core driver for these characters, and the need to unlock the mystery of another character can be a powerful force that draws them together.

This genre also requires some identity-level exploration. The Nerd or Bookworm has rooted their identity and personality for so long in that label, and the idea that someone sees them outside of that safe space is terrifying and—in many cases—unbelievable. They've been told, perhaps from a very young age, that they are unique, weird, odd, brilliant, different, strange. They simply don't fit into the norm. And though they might have a group of wonderful friends who accept them, they still believe that they aren't what anyone would be looking for in a partner.

BREAKDOWN OF ARCHETYPES

Creative genius—Likely to be relatively scatter-brained, messy, lost in daydreams, and struck with brilliant ideas at inconvenient times that they then dive into, often losing track of time and meals. These characters overlap with the Eccentric trope and tend to be the male main character—a.k.a. "The Quirky Genius Smart Guy," but it may also be the eccentric artist, locking herself away in her room to paint until her heartbreak disappears.

265

Methodical genius—Extremely logical, detail oriented, analytical, and precise. Once these methodical Geniuses have identified a problem, they'll become obsessed until we find the answer.

Bookworm—Less likely to be drawn toward new ideas and solutions, the Bookworm (or Bookish Nerd) is far more likely to desire to live in other worlds, appreciating the magic and wonder that other people have built. Their "preferred" intellectual escape may not be fiction, but could also be art, music, or history. These characters tend to be the heroine, a.k.a. the "Bookish Smart Girl."

Geeky nerd—These characters are ultra passionate about something that is generally regarded as unpopular or strange. These are the characters obsessed with comic books or a specific genre of movie. They may have a close-knit group of friends who share their interest but will for the most part avoid or be excluded by those who don't appreciate the same things.

All of these archetypes will cause your character to prefer their own company (or the company of their books) over the dull everyday goings-on around them. It is your other character who will slowly make them realize that there is nothing boring about true love.

COMMON PITFALLS

Makeover/personality change solving everything: As our characters grow throughout the story and re-evaluate their identity, it may result in changes to their appearance. They may take more care with their clothing or experiment with how makeup makes them feel. However, if a personality transplant or a sudden makeover is what makes the love interest perk up and pay attention, we've missed the entire point: the Nerd or Bookworm character has ALWAYS been desirable and more than good enough.

266

Condescension: For extremely intelligent characters, conversations with "normies" can border on painful. However smart your character is, it will be hard to redeem them if they are constantly condescending to other people in their life. A character can be the smartest person in the room without making everyone else feel stupid. If your character grows in this area throughout the story, make sure it is genuine and gradual, and that their intentions shine through in each situation. If their blunt or tactless put-downs are entirely unintentional (such as a character who struggles with reading social cues), how they respond to finding out that they offend people should be handled with care.

Inconsistent type of genius: At the danger of stereotyping, it is likely that your character will fall into one of the Archetypes listed above. If they have characteristics of more than one, it may feel inconsistent and unbelievable or over the top to the reader, as it is unlikely that your character truly excels at *everything* they do.

COMMONLY PAIRED TROPES

The Genius/Nerd/Bookworm trope is commonly paired with Opposites Attract (specifically, a powerful/confident man paired with a Bookworm heroine). The Nerd is often also an Eccentric Billionaire, who amassed their fortune through invention and intellectual pursuit and likely has little interest in enjoying the fruits of their labor.

This character is also often paired with tropes that force them to reevaluate their priorities or humanize their superior intellect such as Instant Family, Marriage of Convenience, Damsel in Distress, or Friends to Love.

267

POTENTIAL WOUNDS

Social difficulties
Being bullied
Being humiliated by others
Being raised by parents who loved conditionally
Having one's ideas or work stolen
Being let down by a trusted organization or social system
Cracking under pressure

COMMON TRAITS

Outcast	Introverted	Logical
Intelligent	Inquisitive	Studious
Shy	Detail oriented	Organized
Curious	Awkward	Scattered
Precise	Daydreamer	Devoted
Passionate	Analytical	Dynamic

POLITICIAN

THIS TROPE FULFILLS THE READER'S DESIRE FOR A HERO WHO IS INFLUENTIAL AND CHARMING

The Politician trope involves at least one central character who holds a position in politics, government, or public service. This character is typically intelligent, charismatic, and *influential*. Politician stories typically explore topics such as ethics, ambition, authenticity, and the intersection of public image and private life.

These characters are dedicated to their career, working to make positive changes in the world through policy, advocacy, and public service. Their position of power and influence often makes them a prominent figure in their community or on a larger stage.

Politicians may work at the local, state, or federal level, but the dynamics of expectations and responsibility should reflect this. For example, if your politician is mayor, unless he oversees a major city, he isn't going to make the national news, but his scandals may become the talk of his small-town and seriously hamper his ability to make productive change or pursue the love interest.

Examples of political offices that may be used in this trope include:

- President
  - Royalty and other heads of state would also likely fit this trope
- Cabinet positions (such as Vice President, Secretary of State or Chief of Staff)

POLITICIAN

- Senator or Congressman
- Mayor
- Political lobbyist or activist
- Political aides

WHY READERS LOVE IT

There is no doubt that a character who has world-changing goals and ambition is worthy of admiration—and the occasional swoon. These characters work hard to maintain their position and avoid scandal. Their reputation is everything—which sometimes leads them astray.

The Politician trope offers readers an intriguing mix of drama, power dynamics, and character growth within the romance narrative. The clash between a character's political endeavors and romantic pursuits leads to compelling conflict and emotional tension that captivates readers.

The stakes are high in these political careers—at least, they should always *feel* high to the reader. Depending on their specific position or the political climate, these characters may face physical risk or dangers due to their involvement in politics. This element is used frequently in stories with a suspense component.

READER EXPECTATIONS

As public figures, Politicians often face scrutiny from the media, the community, or their constituents. This should have some impact on their personal lives and romantic relationships, adding external pressure and contributing to personal and relational conflict. In many ways, this trope overlaps with the Celebrity.

This trope comes wrought with scheming opponents, skeletons in the closet, backroom deals, power struggles, *and* sacrifice—setting the stage for plenty of tension for your readers to feast on. Yet your characters should still be relatable, and if they come from differing ideological backgrounds, they should learn to accept and appreciate each other's differences, finding common ground and a way to connect.

The conflict between maintaining a public image and fostering a genuine personal connection can lead to misunderstandings, secrets, and even betrayal. While readers expect the Politician to be torn between a sense of duty and their pursuit of romance, they should treat both with the weight they deserve. If your character is romantic *without* consideration to their political career or constantly chooses their job above the love interest, readers will doubt the competence of your politician or the depth of the relationship.

COMMON PITFALLS

Imbalance of power: While much of the allure of these characters lies in their ability to influence, be sure not to let them overexert this influence without consequence. The power dynamics inherent in this trope can raise concerns about coercion and manipulation. Be sure that you establish the relationship between these characters as being one based on mutual respect and admiration.

Too many trust issues: The secrecy, compromises and, for lack of a better word, politicking required of the Politician can lead to trust issues between characters. Be sure that readers can both empathize with the difficult circumstances of being in a loving relationship with such a character while also establishing a solid basis of trust and transparency between the love interests wherever possible.

POLITICIAN

Politics: Consider avoiding especially divisive and relevant political topics if you want to avoid frustrating readers. While your goal may be to shed new light on a controversial topic or focus on a topic that is dear to your heart, be aware that you will run the risk of receiving backlash and negative reviews for talking about any subjects when your reader is likely to come to the table with an opinion. For readers who pick up romance as an escape from real-life problems and drama, the political context might also feel too close to reality and detract from your reader's ability to engage with the narrative.

COMMONLY PAIRED TROPES

Due to the very public nature of most political offices, the Politician is often paired with the Celebrity trope. Social events, media attention, and high-profile characters make this trope rife with opportunity for all the glitz and glamour of the Celebrity trope.

Given the likelihood of public scrutiny and expectations, political rivalry, and ideological conflict in the Politician's life, tropes such as Forbidden Love and Enemies to Lovers easily mix. The love interest may be considered off-limits due to ethics or political affiliations, creating a sense of urgency, charged interactions, and emotional intensity in the narrative.

This trope is also often combined with Royalty, leaning into the political power of the office. Or, in the opposite vein, small town politics can have all the impact on a smaller scale. Because these heroes are so passionate about their beliefs, it is very common for the Opposites Attract trope to be used, pairing your politician with a partner who disagrees with them in some major way.

The celebrity and influential status of some politicians means that the Bodyguard trope has plenty of opportunity to come to the forefront.

Lastly, because reputation and public opinion of politicians is paramount, tropes that are dishonest about the relationship tend to feel believable. Hidden Relationship, Secret Baby, Fake Relationship, or Marriage of Convenience are all examples of such tropes that threaten the reputation of the politician and are therefore tantalizing to readers.

POTENTIAL WOUNDS

Suffered or witnessed an injustice
Family estrangement
Loss of a loved one
Betrayal by colleague
Failed idealism
Past scandal or mistake

COMMON TRAITS

Charismatic	Calculating	Compromising
Ambitious	Idealistic	Articulate
Diplomatic	Manipulative	Shrewd
Strategic	Visionary	Resilient
Persuasive	Cunning	Confident

Part Four

CASE STUDIES

CASE STUDY 1

LOVE AND HONOR (2013)

MEN IN UNIFORM

PLAYBOY

SLACKER

ABOUT THE MOVIE

LOVE AND HONOR
Starring:
> Liam Hemsworth as Mickey Wright
> Austin Stowell as Dalton Joiner
> Teresa Palmer as Candace
> Aimee Teegarden as Juniper/Jane
> Chris Lowell as Peter

Release date: March 22, 2013 (USA)
Director: Danny Mooney
Screenplay: Garrett K. Schiff, Jim Burnstein

FEATURED TROPES

Character Tropes: Man in Uniform, Playboy, Slacker
Relational Tropes: Opposites Attract
Situational Tropes: Hidden Identity
Setting Tropes: Historical (Vietnam era)

SYNOPSIS

Private First Class Mickey Wright and PFC Dalton Joiner serve in the same unit in Vietnam. Joiner is revealed to be a master at uncovering Viet Cong booby traps, a skill apparently fostered by his all-consuming desire to return home to his beloved girlfriend, Jane. Following a harrowing encounter with enemy forces and subsequent evacuation, the unit is granted a week of rest and recuperation in Hong Kong. Seizing this opportunity, Joiner decides to utilize his extended leave to return to the United States and win back Jane's heart after she sent a Dear John letter, with Wright choosing to accompany him on this journey.

LOVE AND HONOR

Upon their arrival in Ann Arbor, the two soldiers are confronted with a surprising revelation: Jane has transformed into a free-spirited hippie who now goes by the name Juniper. She resides in a communal house alongside fellow college students who are deeply entrenched in the counterculture movement, among them the captivating Candace. Since the soldiers are not exactly welcomed by these anti-war activists putting out an underground newspaper, the fast-talking Wright spins a tale about their decision to desert the Army in protest of the war. Their supposed act of defiance earns them a hero's welcome among the activists, who view them as symbols of resistance against the conflict. At an antiwar protest, they are outed as deserters and the police begin searching for them.

Candace and the charismatic activist leader, Peter, plan to write a feature story centered on Wright and Joiner. Joiner and Juniper's relationship takes a serious turn with an engagement, and he confesses the truth about their non-desertion to her. The engagement celebration takes an unexpected turn when Joiner witnesses Juniper kissing another man, leading to their breakup. Meanwhile, a genuine connection forms between Candace and Wright. As the search for the "deserters" intensifies, Candace stumbles upon Wright's deception regarding the true nature of their return to the states.

The soldiers are headed to the airport, but they turn around so Wright can go win back Candace. While he is at the house, the police come and arrest him. Joiner manages to free Wright by pretending to be the Military Police and they go to the airport, where Joiner announces he isn't going back to Vietnam. Wright returns, but not before Candace finds him in the airport and promises to wait for him.

KEY TROPES, READER WISH FULFILLMENT, AND ANALYSIS

MEN IN UNIFORM (MILITARY)—reader's desire for brave and dedicated heroes

While both Joiner and Wright are Military heroes, they are very different from each other. Specifically, Wright has the Playboy and Slacker tropes going on as well. The paradox of Military being a trope that thrives on dedication and the Slacker being one that almost excludes the trait means Wright has a lot of growing up to do.

We get to see him do it throughout the movie. The historical setting of Vietnam is an especially good place for this complex character. Even at the conclusion of the movie, his character's commitment is not to the military or to the war, it is to his squad.

In the end, it is Wright's determination to honor his word and serve his time in Vietnam that makes you grow in respect for him. Without that grounding, admirable trait, Wright is just a character that has otherwise been busy the whole movie cracking jokes and hitting on women.

MEN-IN-UNIFORM KEY QUOTES

Joiner: Over there, without Jane, I'm dead.
Wright: Yeah? What about the guys, Joiner? Franklin, Sanchez, Burns, me for C****t's sakes? You desert all of us too. Don't you think I know what you're feeling? Do you know how badly I want to run off with Candace? I'd be happy as hell to run off to some

damn farm in Canada. But I'm not. Cause it's Tuesday in Hong Kong and we're going back tonight. End of story.

***

Wright: You made a commitment. Not to win a war, but to the squad and we're counting on our point man to lead us home alive. Why the hell do you think I got on that plane?

PLAYBOY—reader's desire to be pursued by a charming hero who could have anyone he wants

Mickey Wright is clearly experienced at charming women. In the movie, we see it in the way he flirts with not one, but two stewardesses on the first flight. They practically fawn over him. Later in the movie, he tries to use a very similar tactic to hit on Candace, but she doesn't fall for it—and we love her for it. It takes a little while for Candace to trust him, then that trust is shattered when she finds out he's been lying the entire time.

But, as promised, we get to see Wright grow in this area. Most notably, the screenwriters intentionally showcased his transformation in two ways. On the flight home, the stewardess clearly wants to pick up where they left off a week prior, but Wright doesn't engage beyond polite conversation.

Then, when he is talking to his squad, they are asking for the crazy story (because he usually tells them) and he doesn't share anything. Instead, he's busy writing a letter to Candace. It was a really powerful way to show that the man who met Candace was not the same person who left her in the airport after a week.

PLAYBOY KEY QUOTES

Joiner: Do you ever stop to think before you just let your bull****
fly?
Wright: No, not really.

***

Wright: You think I got a chance with that Candace?
Joiner: Honestly? No.
Wright: I was hoping you'd say that.

**SLACKER—reader's desire to see love bring out the passion
and potential of their partner**

Wright is a bit of a class clown. He's charming and fast-talking,
constantly weaving stories to the point where you can't tell where
the truth stops and the fiction begins. Whereas PFC Joiner
volunteered for the war, Wright was drafted. He volunteered to be
the radio man because it is the safest place in the squad—right in
the middle.

It is interesting to compare the behavior of the two friends at the
beginning of the movie and the end. At the beginning, Joiner is
serious and focused while Wright is joking and making light of the
war. At the end, it is Wright who is serious and committed, while
Joiner has chosen to make their temporary AWOL a more
permanent situation by officially deserting.

At the end of the movie, though, we see that Wright has taken over
Joiner's place as point-man, looking for traps and leading the squad.
It is another representation of him stepping away from his devil-
may-care ways and shouldering more responsibility.

SLACKER KEY QUOTES

Wright: Will you lighten up? It's a party!

***

Joiner: Hey, stay out of trouble.
Wright: Where's the fun in that?

***

Wright: I've never been committed to a damn thing in my whole life. Not school. Not the war. Until now.

CASE STUDY 2

FOREVER MY GIRL (2018)

CELEBRITY/ROCK STAR

BAD BOY

SINGLE PARENT

ABOUT THE MOVIE

Forever My Girl
Starring:
      Alex Roe as Liam Page
      Jessica Rothe as Josie
      John Benjamin Hickey as Pastor Brian Page
      Abby Ryder Fortson as Billy
      Peter Cambor as Sam
Release Date: January 19, 2018
Director: Bethany Ashton Wolf
Screenplay: Bethany Ashton Wolf
Based on: Forever My Girl by Heidi McLaughlin

FEATURED TROPES

Character Tropes: Celebrity/Rock Star, Playboy, Single Parent
Relational Tropes: Second Chance, Secret Baby
Situational Tropes: Jilted Bride, Coming Home
Setting Tropes: Small Town

SYNOPSIS

The movie opens on Josie and Liam's wedding day, showcasing the excitement of the entire town of St. Augustine, Louisiana for the coming nuptials and Liam Page's recent release of his single. Just before the ceremony, Josie receives the news that her groom won't be coming—shattering her entire world.

Eight years later, Liam is bona fide country music star with a Bad Boy reputation. We get a glimpse into his lifestyle of drinking, hotels and women—but he causes quite the stir when he rushes through the French Quarter of New Orleans in his bare feet (followed by adoring fans) to a mobile retail store where he declares, "I'll give anyone ten thousand dollars if they can fix my phone." When the store manager returns his beat-up, duct-taped old cell phone, Liam immediately opens and listens to an eight-year-old voicemail from Josie, sent after he left her at the altar.

In his manager's hotel room, sees a news story about the sudden death of his childhood best friend, Mason. He leaves the hotel room and gets drunk, missing his flight to his next tour location, then bribes his driver to drop him off in St. Augustine without telling anyone where he is. He shows up at the funeral, trying to be discreet, but he is recognized by Josie who promptly punches him in the stomach.

While crashing at his childhood home and attempting to reconnect with Josie, Liam discovers that they have a daughter named Billy. He finds that the town is still bitter about his abrupt departure, and Josie is even more reluctant to trust or forgive him, despite his request to be a part of hers and Billy's life. Realizing the impact of his absence on the lives of those he abandoned, Liam slowly begins healing and learning to appreciate the relationships that truly matter. In the end, he is able to win over Josie, despite his fears that he will never be enough for her or for Billy.

KEY TROPES, READER WISH FULFILLMENT, AND ANALYSIS

CELEBRITY/ROCK STAR—reader's desire to be provided for and cherished above everything else, and for a larger-than-life hero

Throughout the movie, viewers get constant reminders of his celebrity status by townspeople and intervention by his publicist and manager. They have some fun with it early on, with Liam calling his manager for access to a credit card, asking for a car to be sent to him, and getting help with ordering gifts for Billy and Josie.

When Josie asks Liam for a date, he plays up the celebrity, even having his publicist and pop culture networks there to witness their entry into the restaurant. Liam picks her up with a helicopter in a field, takes her for an extravagant dinner where they are met by a swarm of fans, the press, and his publicist. As the movie closes, we see Liam performing with Billy on stage in Germany, with Josie and his father standing backstage.

CELEBRITY KEY QUOTES

Josie: I would love to go on a date with THE Liam Page.
Liam: [hesitates]
Josie: No, come on. I never got to experience that with you. We could get all dressed up, go for a fancy dinner somewhere, drink tons of champagne . . . watch your fans go crazy.

***

Billy: What happened? Why did you leave my mama?
Liam: Well, I was so young. I just—I didn't know how to handle being famous. I guess I just—I got lost. And I got lost for such a long time I couldn't find my way back.

SINGLE PARENT—reader's desire for strong men to embrace the role of fatherhood and love to prevail despite difficult circumstances

Josie is fiercely protective over Billy, the daughter she shares with Liam. Given Liam's history of letting his family down, she is incredibly cautious to trust or rely on him. She is initially hesitant about the idea of letting him spend time with Billy, but after having a conversation with her daughter, who is open to the idea of getting to know her dad, she hesitantly accepts. She is quick to remind Liam at every turn of the responsibility and significance of being a permanent figure in his daughter's life.

As she sees him change and strive to be a good father to Billy, she begins to let herself fall for him anew. The night Billy asks to call Liam Dad, and he lets Josie know that he is ready to stick around, she asks him to take her out on a date.

Billy is an ever-present character in the movie, in fact most of the scenes revolve around her, which really keeps the tension between fear of disappointment and the desire to hope for something more front and center throughout the film. She is a bit overly precocious, but it's somewhat balanced by the fact that she pretty much universally acknowledged as being remarkable. Every adult in the film has a line about how impressed or surprise they are by her . . . and we have to say, we kind of buy it.

SINGLE PARENT KEY QUOTES

Liam: Billy just asked if she could call me Dad.
Josie: That's a lot of responsibility . . . it's forever, Liam.
Liam: I know. I'm . . . ready.

***

Liam: What kind of music do you want to listen to?
Billie: Um, the only kind there is. Country!
Liam: [Gives Billy a high five] That's my girl.

BAD BOY—reader's desire to be pursued by a hero who could have anyone he wants and to see that love can and does redeem the broken

Truthfully, the execution of this trope was somewhat weak in his characterization. Liam is made into something of a Bad Boy cocktail. He is a little bit of the Slacker, the Rebel, and the Playboy. It is put out really prominently in the first few scenes of the movie. His songs reference whiskey, he is constantly seen drinking, and he is established as indulging in casual relationships with groupies. When he goes to see his manager after fixing his cell phone, he is railed on for failing to produce any material for a new album. It is also mentioned that he has caused problems and delays by not being where he needs to be during tours.

However, they did hit the redemption arc solidly with one twist—while most Bad Boy redemption arcs have a strong influence by the hero's pursuit of his love interest, Liam's is almost entirely driven by his developing bond with Billy and his desire to be a father. Ultimately, it is made clear that he has changed for the benefit of himself and the opportunity of a future with Billy *and* Josie.

BAD BOY KEY QUOTES

Liam: Did you see that blonde in the front row?
Sam: Already on it. Jack's put her in the car, headed to the afterparty.
Liam: Just have a bottle of vodka sent up to my room—and a steak.

***

Liam's dad: I even went backstage to see you after . . . And there you were. You were so out of your mind on God knows what, I honestly thought I'd stumbled into the wrong room. And even after that, I still tried to tell you about Billy.
Liam: I don't remember any of that.
Liam's dad: Yeah, you don't? Why don't I refresh your memory? You told me to leave and never come back . . . The guy I saw in Seattle that night. I knew that Billy and Josie were just better off without him.

CASE STUDY 3

THE AMERICAN PRESIDENT (1995)

CELEBRITY

POLITICIAN

WIDOWER

SEASONED CHARACTERS

SINGLE PARENT

ABOUT THE MOVIE

The American President
Starring:
      Michael Douglas as US President Andrew Shepherd
      Annette Bening as Sydney Wade
      Martin Sheen as AJ MacInerney
      David Paymer as Leon Kodak
      Samantha Mathis as Janie Basdin
      Michael J. Fox as Lewis Rothschild
Release Date: November 17, 1995
Director: Rob Reiner
Screenplay: Aaron Sorkin

FEATURED TROPES

Character Tropes: Celebrity/Politician, Single Parent, Widower,
Seasoned Characters
Relational Tropes: None
Situational Tropes: None
Setting Tropes: Workplace Romance

SYNOPSIS

President Andrew Shepherd is preparing to run for re-election, and
chances of a successful bid are boosted by his high approval rating
and a moderate crime control bill that is his highest priority in
policy. Shepherd is determined to announce the bill—with all the
support lined up in Congress—by the State of the Union address.

On the personal side, Shepherd is a widower and single father.
Sparks fly when he meets Sydney Ellen Wade, a lobbyist working
to pass fossil fuel reduction legislation. During a meeting, Shepherd

strikes a deal with Sydney: if she can secure 24 votes for the environmental bill before his State of the Union address, he will deliver the last 10 votes.

Shepherd and Sydney begin seeing each other and they fall in love, despite the scrutiny when the relationship is made public. Senator Bob Rumson, who is eyeing the presidency, homes in on Sydney's history as an activist while casting doubt on Shepherd's morals and family values. As Shepherd chooses not to counter Rumson's allegations, his approval ratings decline, jeopardizing vital political backing and putting the crime bill at risk.

Sydney manages to secure the necessary votes for the environmental bill, leaving Shepherd just three votes shy. His only option is to temporarily set aside the environmental bill in order to secure the support of three Michigan congressmen for the crime bill—a choice he reluctantly makes. Subsequently, Sydney is dismissed from her position at the firm. She confronts Shepherd, ending their relationship and announcing her departure from DC. While he stands by the crime bill as his primary concern, she critiques it for lacking the strength to effectively combat crime.

Prior to the State of the Union address, Shepherd makes a surprise appearance in the White House press room. He counters Rumson's attacks on his values and character, as well as the relentless innuendos that Sydney prostituted herself for political favors. He declares he will send the controversial environmental bill to Congress with the 20% cut in fossil fuels, honoring the deal he made with Sydney. Additionally, he is withdrawing the crime bill for a stronger one with significant gun control measures.

Shepherd and Sydney reconcile, then she walks him to the doors of the House chamber where he enters to thunderous applause as he is about to deliver the State of the Union address.

KEY TROPES,
READER WISH FULFILLMENT,
AND ANALYSIS

CELEBRITY—reader's desire to be provided for and cherished above everything else and for a larger-than-life hero

Despite his status, Andrew Shepherd goes out of his way to be thoughtful. He tries multiple times to send her flowers (not through his assistant!), which leads to some funny moments. He doesn't have credit cards, and the flower shop thinks he's pranking them or faints when he shows up in person. Finally, he gets her flowers from the Rose Garden at the White House the night of the State of the Union.

There are also some serious escapism scenes in this movie, where Sydney accompanies the President to a State Dinner (their first date) or to Camp David for the weekend. At the State Dinner, Sydney is very clearly impressed with the fanfare and glamour. But she also holds her own, making a connection with the French President and his wife by speaking to them in French. It's a little acknowledgement that while Sydney doesn't typically operate in his world now, she could easily do so.

Optics are important and once the media get involved, his approval ratings go way down. His political strategist offers to run new polling numbers to see if dating was a good choice. Shepherd doesn't care about the optics and refuses until the very end, when those same polling numbers make him decide to go back on the deal with Sydney and the fossil fuel bill.

CELEBRITY KEY QUOTES

Sydney: Two hundred pairs of eyes are focused on you right now with two questions in mind: Who is this girl and why is the president dancing with her?

***

Shepherd: I'm just a guy asking a girl over for dinner . . .
[Marine One touches down outside the oval office behind them.]

POLITICIAN—reader's desire for a hero who is influential and charming

All cards on the table, Shepherd is seriously charming. He's really funny and smart—lots of witty banter! And once Sydney gets beyond the "I'm talking to the President" nerves, the two of them have amazing chemistry.

Throughout the movie, one of his closest confidants is his chief of staff, AJ. He repeatedly tries to get AJ to call him "Andy" when they are talking casually, but he won't—even though they've been friends for decades. This comes full circle when Sydney calls him Andy just before they make love.

One of the best parts of this movie is the meet cute. Sydney is in a meeting with her back to the door and ends up absolutely railing on the President's stand on the environmental bill. He walks in halfway through her diatribe. She, of course, is mortified and convinced she's going to lose her job. Still, while she apologizes for her delivery, she never backs down on her stances. She thinks he's going to penalize her firm. Instead, he calls and asks her on a date. This meet cute was especially effective because he's used to everyone kowtowing to him and treading so carefully. Her candor was a breath of fresh air and he just had to know more.

POLITICIAN KEY QUOTES

Sydney: Well, then, your boss is the chief executive of Fantasy Land!

***

Sydney: How did you get this number?
Shepherd: Oh, I don't know . . . FBI, maybe?

SINGLE PARENT—reader's desire for strong men to embrace the role of fatherhood and love to prevail despite difficult circumstances

Lucy Shepherd does fall into a bit of the "perfect child" in this film. Her scenes are limited, but important for the characterization of her father. They have a great rapport, and it is obvious that he loves her and makes her a priority, despite the fact that he is the leader of the free world. He talks about a parent-teacher conference and encourages her to get more excited about Social Studies.

Shepherd also has the pretty critical conversation with his daughter before his first date, making sure she is okay with him going out with a woman. She gives him the green light, and when she meets Sydney later on, you can tell she is a fan of the relationship progressing.

SINGLE PARENT KEY QUOTES

Lucy: Do you see it as part of your job to torture me?
Shepherd: No, just one of the perks
Lucy: [plays "Hail to the Chief" on her trombone as he leaves the room]

***

Sydney [referring to Lucy]: She's wonderful.
Shepherd: She's her mother.
Sydney: She's you.

WIDOWER—reader's desire for love to overcome loss

The movie starts off with very fast-paced happenings in the West Wing of the White House. When the President's cousin can't accompany him to the state dinner, he says he'll just go stag. One of his staffers replies without thinking, suggesting that looking like the lonely widower is never a bad move. He doesn't take it well, and she immediately apologizes. But it is the comment that starts his mind moving toward the idea of no longer being the widower.

The timeline isn't super well-defined in the movie, but the dialogue indicates that his wife died sometime about a year before the presidential campaign—which means about 5 years ago. It is obvious that Andy loved and misses his wife, but his charming and humorous personality takes center stage. We have to wonder if we would see more inner turmoil about the "moving on" stage if this had been a book. But as it stands, he pursues Sydney Wade wholeheartedly from the moment he decides that he is interested.

WIDOWER KEY QUOTES

Press Secretary: We've never gone wrong parading you around as the lonely widower.

***

Shepherd: I've loved two women in my life. I lost one to cancer, and I lost the other 'cause I was so busy keeping my job I forgot to do my job. Well, that ends right now.

295

SEASONED CHARACTERS—reader's desire to know that it is never too late to find true love

The main characters in this story have very different back stories. Sydney has never been married, always choosing her career over relationships. Shepherd, on the other hand, has been married and widowed.

In either case, they are quite self-aware about the unusual nature of their relationship—even poking fun at the perceived oddity of flirting, dating, and navigating a relationship at their age.

Both characters are straight-forward and confident about what they want. Shepherd pursues Sydney from the beginning and Sydney is very decisive when she invites him to bed instead of going with his suggested slower timeline. When they have conflict, both of them face it head-on. There is no silent treatment or dishonesty, both comfortable and willing to hash out the issue, even when they are hurting.

SEASONED CHARACTERS KEY QUOTES

Shepherd: So, she didn't say anything about me?
AJ: Well, no, but I could pass her a note before study hall.

***

[After Sydney hangs up on him thinking it was a prank call]
Shepherd: This used to be easier.

CASE STUDY 4

THE LONGEST RIDE

COWBOY

ATHLETE

CREATIVE GENIUS

ABOUT THE MOVIE

The Longest Ride
Starring:
      Britt Robertson as Sophia Danko Collins
      Scott Eastwood as Luke Collins
      Jack Huston as Young Ira
      Oona Chaplin as Young Ruth
      Jason Fabian
      Alan Alda as Ira Levinson
Release Date: April 10, 2015
Directed by   George Tillman, Jr.
Written by   Craig Bolotin
Based on   The Longest Ride by Nicholas Sparks

FEATURED TROPES

Character Tropes: Cowboy, Athlete (Rodeo Cowboy), Creative Genius
Relational Tropes: Opposites Attract
Situational Tropes: None
Setting Tropes: Small Town, Split Timeline

SYNOPSIS

Luke Collins, a professional bull rider (PBR), crosses paths with art student Sophia Danko, at a PBR event. After their first date, they save an elderly man, Ira Levinson, from a car crash. Sophia pulls a treasure trove of love letters from the wreckage.

As Sophia visits the hospital-bound Ira, she volunteers to read aloud the letters he wrote to his late wife, Ruth. The letters become a window into the past, recounting the poignant tale of Ruth and Ira's deepening affection amid the backdrop of World War II.

Delving into flashbacks, Ruth and Ira's love story unfolds. A desire for a big family unites them, but war separates them, testing their bond. Ira's injury leaves them unable to have children, straining their relationship, yet they decide to weather the storm. Their shared love for art brings them closer, turning their home into a gallery of cherished memories.

In the present day, Ira's health necessitates his move to a nursing home. Sophia's visits persist as Luke continues his bull riding career, and their affection deepens into love. While attending an art exhibit, the disparities between their worlds emerge starkly, leading them both to question the viability of their relationship.

Sophia seeks solace and wisdom from Ira, who imparts lessons from his own life with Ruth. Flashbacks unveil a heartrending chapter of Ruth's attachment to a young student named Daniel, revealing the void left by their inability to adopt him.

As Luke sustains an injury while bull riding, his determination to continue riding despite the risk results in a painful breakup. Simultaneously, past events reveal a temporary separation between Ruth and Ira due to their differing views on children. Their eventual reunion and the passage of time bring with them the inevitable reality of Ruth's passing.

A knock on Ira's door heralds the arrival of a woman bearing news of Daniel's passing and a portrait of Ruth. The portrait holds a heartfelt inscription from Daniel, encapsulating Ruth's impact as his teacher and mentor.

In the present, Ira's passing prompts an auction of his valuable art collection. Meanwhile, Luke conquers his final bull ride and championship, but the triumph rings hollow without Sophia by his side.

At the auction, Luke purchases the painting by Daniel, "Portrait of Ruth." Sophia and Luke reconcile, as he articulates his desire to prioritize a life with Sophia over his bull riding career. After the purchase, the auctioneer reveals a secret clause in Ira's will that stipulates the buyer of Ruth's portrait would receive the entire collection. A year later, Luke and Sophia marry, creating an art gallery dedicated to Ira and Ruth's legacy.

KEY TROPES, READER WISH FULFILLMENT, AND ANALYSIS

COWBOY—reader's desire for heroes who are hardworking and rooted in family and traditional values

There are tons of reader-favorite cowboy scenes in this movie. Luke is portrayed as a down-home, wholesome cowboy, despite his pursuit of the PBR title. A few of the specific examples would be how when she calls him, he's busy stacking firewood. He brings her flowers, picks her up, and their first date is a picturesque picnic by the lake with barbecue takeout. Sophia mentions more than once that she's never had a date like that before.

Luke's relationship with his mother is at the forefront of his motivations. He's convinced himself that he keeps riding so he can earn money to take care of his mother, now that his dad is gone. His mom challenges him on that motivation repeatedly, insisting that he should quit.

Luke and Sophia spend a lot of time at the ranch, horseback riding and looking at his baby pictures. Aside from the tough, competitive Athlete side that comes from the Rodeo pursuit, Luke Collins is still a traditional, family-focused Cowboy at heart.

COWBOY KEY QUOTES

Sophia: I saw the way those girls stared at you.
Luke: And you think I'm that kind of guy?

***

Sophia: So it's all about winning?
Luke: No, it's not all about winning. Well, not entirely. I've got a family ranch, and it's been a tough couple of years. My mom is kind of all on her own. I've just got to keep making money.

ATHLETE (RODEO COWBOY ARCHETYPE)—reader's desire to see passion, competence, discipline, and strength in their partner

The movie kicks off with a scene showing just how tough Luke Collins is. The crowd is cheering, the announcer is talking up his accomplishments, three-time world champion bull rider that he is. But Luke gets thrown and seriously injured. The rest of the movie shows Luke trying to climb his way back up the PBR leader board, despite the doctors' and his mother's insistence that it isn't safe after his injuries.

Luke isn't just competitive and driven, he is determined to compete despite everyone telling him it is reckless. We repeatedly see Luke popping painkillers and hobbling in pain. He has scars from where the bull gored him.

Several times, we see flashbacks of the incident where he was hurt, and Rango (the bull) makes several appearances that shake Luke up. Rango is portrayed as the unbeatable enemy, an unrideable bull. When Luke finally competes and wins the world title at the end of the movie, it is Rango that he has to ride. It is the ultimate victory—redemption over the bull who defeated him before. It's everything Luke thought he wanted, but the victory falls flat as he looks to the stands where there is no Sophia cheering him on.

ATHLETE KEY QUOTES

Another rider (Jared): You had a good night, but it's a long way back to the top.

***

Sophia: What about you? What's your story?
Luke: Mine's pretty simple. Just keep winning events. Make it to the top thirty-five. Go to Vegas. Make it to the finals. I've got some making up to do.

***

Luke: Well, all bull riders get hurt. It's not if, it's when. And how bad.

CREATIVE GENIUS/ARTIST—reader's desire to be accepted as they are, for their brain as well as their beauty

Throughout the movie, Sophia is portrayed as ambitious and studious, and passionate about art. She has a prestigious internship lined up with a gallery in Manhattan. Her friends have to cajole her to skip studying to attend the rodeo with them.

Luke's hat falls off in front of her in the stands and she offers it back to him, but he tells her to keep it as they share a moment. This is a good example of giving him a reason to focus in on her in a sea of other people, and it gives them a connection point when they see each other at the honky-tonk after the rodeo.

There are multiple instances where Luke affirms that Sophia is special and different from the other girls he has known. They discuss their pasts and that she is the child of immigrants, bemoaning the difficulties of standing out from the crowd.

Her high-brow passion for art is a delicious place for contrast between these two characters. Examples include Luke walking across campus for her in his boots and plaid shirt to stares from other students and sighs of admiration from her sorority house. Or Luke in his jeans and boots, rubbing shoulders with rich art snobs at the gallery event.

CREATIVE GENIUS KEY QUOTES

Sophia: I just . . . I love art. I love everything about it. I love studying it. I love the culture that it brings and the whole human experience. Just all wrapped up into one, you know? Anger, sadness, love, passion, history . . .

***

Sophia: I always wanted to be like everyone else when I was little.

Luke: The reason I like you is because you're nothing like everyone else.

***

Sophia's boss: What did you think of tonight?
Luke: Honestly?
Sophia's boss: Of course.
Luke: I think there is more bull**** here than where I work.

CASE STUDY 5

10 THINGS I HATE ABOUT YOU

BAD BOY/ REBEL GIRL

GRUMP

ABOUT THE MOVIE

10 Things I Hate About You

Starring:

      Julia Stiles as Kat Stratford

      Heath Ledger as Patrick Verona

      Joseph Gordon-Levitt as Cameron James

      Larisa Oleynik as Bianca Stratford

      Larry Miller as Walter Stratford

      Andrew Keegan as Joey Donner

      David Krumholtz as Michael Eckman

Release Date: March 31, 1999

Directed by   Gil Junger

Written by   Karen McCullah and Kirsten Smith

Based on   *The Taming of the Shrew* by William Shakespeare

FEATURED TROPES

Character Tropes: Bad Boy, Rebel Girl, The Grump

Relational Tropes: Enemies to Lovers

Situational Tropes: Hidden Motivations/Incentive, Forced Proximity

Setting Tropes: High School

SYNOPSIS

The film begins with Cameron James, a new student, who instantly falls for the beautiful and popular Bianca Stratford. However, Bianca's strict and overprotective father has a rule that she can only date if her older, more rebellious sister, Kat, does. The problem is that Kat has a reputation for being outspoken, independent, and uninterested in dating, which makes her an unlikely candidate for romance.

Cameron seeks the help of another student, Michael, who goes with him to approach Patrick Verona, an enigmatic and rebellious student. When Patrick refuses to ask Kat out, Michael convinces him to enlist Joey Donner (a jock who wants to date Kat's sister) in order to pay Patrick to date Kat. Patrick agrees to the plan, and the story follows his efforts to win over Kat, despite her initial resistance.

As Patrick spends time with Kat, they gradually develop genuine feelings for each other. At the same time, Cameron tries to win Bianca's affection by pretending to know French and helping her with her schoolwork. After a party, Cameron confesses his true feelings to Bianca, who realizes her own feelings for him.

As the relationships become more complicated, the characters must confront their true emotions and deal with the consequences of their actions. This culminates when Kat discovers that Patrick was paid to date her during prom, causing a rift between them. Ultimately, Kat forgives Patrick, and Bianca ends up with Cameron.

KEY TROPES, READER WISH FULFILLMENT, AND ANALYSIS

BAD BOY/REBEL GIRL—reader's desire to break free from societal norms and expectations

Both Kat and Patrick fall solidly into the Bad Boy/Rebel category, making them an interesting, yet wildly entertaining couple. It is also what sets them apart among their peers. They both have a strong nonconformist attitude. Neither cares much about fitting in, and Kat especially is very opposed to fulfilling society norms and expectations.

Kat is portrayed as independent, an individual thinker, and assertive—much of the time these characteristics are used to voice her feminist-leaning opinions. These feminist beliefs are a fairly significant part of her reputation. She is unapologetic about her views on gender equality and women's rights, and her interests almost entirely align with this worldview—from bands, to literature, to pastimes. This is demonstrated in the way she challenges traditional gender roles, resists authority figures, and is willing to speak her mind—even when it gets her kicked out of class or sent to the counselor's office.

Kat is somewhat of an outsider at school, which adds to her rebellious image. She's not part of the popular crowd and loudly detests the interests and pursuits of her fellow students. She doesn't care about social hierarchy or popularity contests, and she rejects the idea of conforming to cliques at the expense of her principles. At one point she sits down with her sister, Bianca, to caution her about falling into the same trap she did when she was dating the very same student Bianca is interested in. Like with any good rebel character, these moments of tenderness and vulnerability are key to creating a satisfying character arc.

Patrick is certainly a rebel in his own right, but he is slightly more mysterious to the student population, with many of the rumors told about him turning out to be untrue. His sardonic sense of humor and sarcasm seem to scare others away, further adding to his mystique.

He is fiercely independent, but he does seem to care slightly more what others think about him, as opposed to Kat. Multiple times in the movie he makes remarks like, "I can't be seen there," or "Don't say [stuff] like that out loud, people can hear you." Despite this apparent consciousness of his reputation, he clearly does not have any desire to conform to expectations.

While a great many of Patrick's early scenes place him in the counselor's office and bars, skipping class, smoking and engaging in otherwise frowned upon behaviors for a high school senior, there is depth to his character revealed through his other talents, particularly music. He and Kat bond over their love for music and their fondness for the guitar, and in a ploy to win her over, he performs a rendition of Franki Valli's "Can't Take My Eyes Off of You" which results in a hilarious chase scene with the high school security officers.

His caring side comes out as the relationship with Kat unfolds, with him eventually developing genuine feelings for her and attempting to get out of the arrangement before succumbing to the temptation of more money. Patrick is portrayed as a multi-dimensional character who starts as a typical Rebel but gradually reveals layers of depth and vulnerability as the story progresses. His character development is an essential part of the film's narrative, making him one of the most memorable characters in the teen romance canon.

BAD BOY/REBEL GIRL KEY QUOTES

[Patrick stabs a frog specimen with his pocketknife while Cameron watches.]
Cameron: Hey, what about him?
Michael: Him? No, no, don't look at him. He's a criminal. I heard

he lit a state trooper on fire. He just did a year in San Quentin. . . . He sold his own liver on the black market to buy a new set of speakers.

***

Patrick: So what's your excuse?
Kat: For?
Patrick: For acting the way that we do.
Kat: I don't like to do what people expect. Why should I live up to anyone else's expectations instead of my own?

***

Patrick: No, none of that stuff is true.
Kat: State trooper?
Patrick: Fallacy. Uh . . . dead guy in the parking lot?
Kat: Rumor. The duck?
Patrick: Hearsay. Bobby Ridgway's balls?
Kat: Fact. But he deserved it. He tried to grope me in the lunch line.
Patrick: Ah, fair enough.

THE GRUMP—reader's desire to intimately know someone that keeps most people at a distance

Kat definitely takes the cake as the loveable grump . . . although it takes some time for most to come around to her abrasive demeanor and acerbic wit. She seemingly has a single friend and generally seems to keep to herself as something of a loner. This self-imposed isolation and her aloof attitude definitely contribute to her grumpy reputation.

Her disinterest in typical social events and parties is made apparent throughout the film, and she often displays this along with a heaping dose of cynicism. She's skeptical of romantic gestures and relationship, based on her response to Patrick's advances, and it

310

contrasts sharply with Bianca's eagerness for social events and a dating life.

It's important to note that Kat's grumpy demeanor is complemented by the more nuanced aspects of her character, especially when it comes to protecting Bianca. This defensiveness often comes off as grumpiness or abrasiveness, as she's quick to challenge anyone who she perceives as a threat. Ultimately, her grumpiness serves as a defense mechanism against the fickle nature of the high school culture and societal expectations which she so staunchly opposes. However, as her relationship with Patrick unfolds, these different facets of her personality are revealed, endearing her to the audience and the other characters.

THE GRUMP KEY QUOTES

School guidance counselor: The point is, Kat . . . people perceive you as somewhat—
Kat: Tempestuous?
Counselor: Heinous b**ch is the term used most often. You might want to work on that.

***

Mr. Stratford: Hello, Katarina. Make anyone cry today?
Kat: Sadly, no. But it's only four-thirty. [smirks]

CASE STUDY 6

THE PRINCE AND ME

ROYALTY

PLAYBOY

BOOKWORM

ABOUT THE MOVIE

The Prince and Me
Starring
     Julia Stiles as Paige Morgan
     Luke Mably as Edvard/Eddie, Crown Prince of Denmark
     Ben Miller as Soren
     Miranda Richardson as Queen consort
     James Fox as King
Release Date: April 2, 2004
Directed by   Martha Coolidge
Written by   Jack Amiel
Michael Begler
Katherine Fugate
Original screenplay by Mark Amin

TROPE HIGHLIGHTS

Character Tropes: Royalty, Playboy, Bookworm
Relational Tropes: Enemies to Lovers
Situational Tropes: Fish Out of Water
Setting Tropes: University

SYNOPSIS

The movie opens by juxtaposing the fast and furious lifestyle of Edvard, the Crown Prince of Denmark, and Paige Morgan's life in small-town Wisconsin. While the prince spends his time street racing and celebrating his victories with a cohort of beautiful women, Paige is so busy working in the lab and focusing on medical school admissions that she barely makes time to attend the wedding of a close friend.

When Edvard decides to escape his royal duties for a taste of ordinary life, he enrolls in Paige's university under a false identity, "Eddie Williams," with only his majordomo Soren accompanying him. Paige and Eddie get off to a poor start when meeting at the bar where Paige works and later when Eddie arrives late to chemistry lab where he proves to be a poor partner to Paige. When she struggles in a class on Shakespeare, Paige asks Eddie to tutor her in exchange for her help at work and in other areas.

During Thanksgiving break, Paige asks Eddie to join her family for the holiday where he is received well by her family. During this time, they share their first kiss and return to the university absolutely smitten with each other.

As they become closer, Paige discovers his true identity and is hesitant to get involved with someone from such a different world. Ultimately her affection for Eddie prevails, and she ends up making a grand gesture by traveling to Denmark to see him. Eddie quickly proposes, at which point Paige is swept up in the chaos and expectations of royal life. When she realizes that she does not fit into this world, she returns home to Wisconsin. After months apart, Eddie returns for her graduation from the university, where he declares his love for her and promises to wait for her to fulfill her dreams before taking her place as his queen.

KEY TROPES, READER WISH FULFILLMENT, AND ANALYSIS

ROYALTY—reader's desire to see love overcome the rules of any society

While many aspects of Edvard's portrayal as Crown Prince felt realistic, like his inclusion in official meetings and his father's desire to guide him into his role, there were some aspects that felt difficult to buy into. For instance, given that this prince is about to become king, it is odd that he has no security when sent to America to go to college. Relying solely on the majordomo for the safety and security of the prince in a foreign land seems like a major oversight.

Once Eddie, as he is called in America, arrives at the university, it is clear that the experience is a serious culture shock to him. His lack of understanding of his financial state leads him to seek work in order to live. This was a good way to humble him and force him to find his way without his family and status taking care of all his wants and needs. When Paige asks Eddie for help with her Shakespeare class, the difference in their experience is highlighted by Eddie asking for help with laundry in return—a task he's never had to accomplish alone.

However, once he lost his entitlement, it happens pretty much with the snap of a finger. He seems to be incredibly grounded very early on in his American experience, and the vast difference in upbringing is barely felt even when he travels to the humble family farm Paige grew up on during Thanksgiving break.

There was a great moment during Thanksgiving dinner when Paige's father discusses the interconnectedness of everyone in society; he is specifically talking about family farms and corporate farms, but Eddie clearly sees the relevance to his own future role as King of Denmark.

Just as they begin to bond, Edvard is revealed to be the prince, and the whirlwind of his royal life begins. Paige is initially strongly opposed to the attention of the press, but once she decides to go all in, Eddie earns her admiration with his strong leadership and willingness to step into his role as future king so abruptly.

ROYALTY KEY QUOTES

Random street racer: Good race, your highness.
Edvard: Yes, well not exactly how I wanted to win. It would have been better if you hadn't lifted your foot off at the end.
Racer: Ah, you did good.

***

Soren: I believe you just got rejected, sir.
Edvard: You know, I don't think that's ever happened to me before.
Soren: You've never been attracted to anyone who didn't know you were a prince before.

***

Edvard: So where do the future king and queen go on their honeymoon?
Paige: I was thinking Morocco.
Edvard: It's really hard to organize security there.
Paige: Oh, right. Okay.
Edvard: What about Spain? . . . I'm sure King Juan Carlos won't mind lending us his private island for a few weeks in the summer.

PLAYBOY—reader's desire to be pursued by a charming hero who could have anyone he wants

Edvard is the typical Bad Boy, arriving late for meetings, barely putting in any effort with his royal duties, and constantly landing himself in scandals. Even during political meetings, he is found doodling and making eyes at the sole woman in the room. In fact, he chooses to go to college after seeing an advertisement for Girls Gone Wild Wisconsin.

His early scenes in Denmark find him surrounded by women, and when he does arrive on campus, he frequently makes comments about the conquests he expects to find there. During his initial meeting with Paige, he sticks his foot in his mouth by assuming that, like the women on Girls Gone Wild, Paige will gladly reveal her body to him at his simple request.

While Eddie's Bad Boy reputation could have easily been used as nothing more than a plot device to get him to the United States, it ends up coming in handy for him when he uses his racing knowledge to win the lawnmower race in Paige's hometown— endearing him further to her family.

He has clearly changed his attitude by the time he and Paige form a connection, as he stops their kiss from advancing and "bids her goodnight." He allows her to initiate intimacy, which ends up happening in the stacks of the university library just before the press discover his presence in the States.

Eddie's change in priorities is evident by the time he returns to Denmark and takes over royal duties for his father. While it is evident to his entire family, it is clear that Paige is truly swayed by this new sense of focus and commitment.

PLAYBOY KEY QUOTES

Eddie: So . . . will you take your top off for me?
Paige: What?
Eddie: Take your top off for me and act like wild college girls. come on nobody's watching, just take it off for me.
[Paige sprays him with the soda tap.]

***

Paige: Are these pictures going to be in the newspaper?
Eddie: Yes
Paige: Are you sure?
Eddie: This isn't my first indiscretion.

NERD—reader's desire to be accepted as they are, for their brain as well as their beauty

Paige is a pre-medical student, and her passion for science is shown from the very first scene where she is working in a lab. It's clear that she struggles to find a balance between her academic pursuits and her personal relationships. When she returns to school, her friends rag her about her unwavering focus and constant thoughts about medical school admissions.

This movie does a good job with the realistic portrayal of the driven, bookish nerd, who are often treated as if they are all around geniuses. While Paige is clearly competent and successful in her scientific and medical-related pursuits, when it comes to Shakespeare, she struggles until Eddie begins helping her.

When Paige reveals her fear of having a life filled with grocery shopping and "picking up the kids from soccer" to her mother, it somewhat foreshadows the dark moment between the couple when she determines that her academic ambitions and future as Queen of Denmark are simply incompatible. Once arriving in Denmark though, Paige initially hesitates to accept her future as Eddie's queen, but she quickly gets wrapped up in the whirlwind of it all.

To some degree, this trope is used as a plot device. While in school, she is clearly focused on performing well and getting into Johns

Hopkins, the best medical school in the country at the time. However, it somewhat disappears as she begins to acclimate to the role of future queen, and it doesn't come back into play until she decides that she can no longer marry Eddie. Whether the character loses herself in the fantasy of it all or whether her character arc simply lacks the depth of Eddie's, it's not entirely clear. In either case, her characterization feels somewhat inconsistent.

NERD KEY QUOTES

Paige [speaking to Edvard]: See, unlike people who are given everything, I have to earn what I get. But that is the beauty of a meritocracy, people rise and fall based on how hard they work.

***

Paige: I'm too busy for distractions.
Paige's mom: Chemistry isn't just in the class, sweetie. And you guys have it.
Paige: Right. Then what happens? I fool myself into thinking he's Prince Charming? We get married and live happily ever after? Then all my work goes down the drain . . .

***

Paige [after telling Edvard she must leave Denmark]: When I first met you, I was so focused because I was scared, and you got me out of that which is the greatest thing anyone has ever done for me. But I'm still me. And all the things that I want to do are still a part of me. And I thought I could make myself forget about that, but I can't.

CASE STUDY 7

HEARTBREAKERS

CHARMER

CINNAMON ROLL

ABOUT THE MOVIE

Heartbreakers
Starring:
>Jennifer Love Hewitt as Page Connors/Jane
>Jason Lee as Jack Withrowe
>Sigourney Weaver as Max Connors/Angela/Ulga
>Gene Hackman as William Tensy
>Ray Liotta as Dean
>Sarah Silverman as Linda
>Zach Galifianakis as Bill

Release Date: March 23, 2001
Directed by   David Mirkin
Written by   Robert Dunn
Paul Guay
Stephen Mazur

TROPE HIGHLIGHTS

Character Tropes: Cinnamon Roll, Charmer
Relational Tropes: Enemies to Lovers
Situational Tropes: Con
Setting Tropes: Beach

SYNOPSIS

As the movie opens, Max Conners is celebrating her wedding day to chop shop owner Dean Cummano, but less than 24 hours into marital bliss, he's conned out of 300,000 dollars when Page, her daughter, seduces him just as Max (under the name Angela) walks into his office.

The women are professionals, conning to avoid paying for absolutely everything—gas, food, hotels—but they are clearly not on the same page about their future working relationship. Page wants to strike out on her own, while her mother warns her that she's not ready to work alone. When they go to withdraw their funds from the bank to split, they are met with an IRS agent threatening to charge them with fraud if they don't pay a considerable sum in back taxes, on top of what was already seized.

The agent is later revealed to be Max's former mentor, and it is obvious that Max is in the habit of manipulating her daughter. Nonetheless, Page agrees to one more partner con, as long as it's on her terms in Palm Beach.

Once they arrive, they begin working on the next target, a tobacco tycoon. Page decides to work a side-con on her own though, a billionaire doctor who is too attached to his elderly mother to indulge in romance. When her attempts to seduce the doctor go awry, she stumbles upon a new target—bartender Jack Withrowe. As the story unfolds, Jack's goodness wins a reluctant Page over and by the time he asks her to marry him, she has developed genuine feelings for him.

She attempts to call her mother off of the con, but when Dean Cummano shows up, discovers their deception, and demands the money they stole from him, Page agrees to follow through. While clearly heartbroken to hurt Jack this way, she goes along with the plan for Max to seduce him on their wedding night. Though in the end, Max must resort to drugging Jack in order to get him in bed with her. In the end, Page finds out what her mother did and returns the deed to Jack's bar, which she received during the divorce settlement. They reunite, and she tells him the truth of her identity.

KEY TROPES,
READER WISH FULFILLMENT,
AND ANALYSIS

CHARMER—reader's desire to be pursued by a charming hero who could have anyone he wants

In something of a gender twist with the Playboy/Charmer trope, Page Conners is a total Casanova. Coupled with the lifelong training she received from her mother on the art of conning, her beauty and brains are a lethal combination.

She becomes more mild-mannered and sweet in the way she talks with him as the relationship develops, even as she is resisting a genuine connection. This demonstrates that Jack is different, she seems him in a way she's never seen men before—ultimately it's his goodness that bursts through her well-built defenses.

Page is beautiful and cunning, and she is depicted as a skilled manipulator, always using her physical beauty and suggestive body language to execute her schemes. She dresses exclusively in tight fitting clothes, always revealing her midriff, an abundant amount of cleavage and typically barely covering her cheeks (and we're not talking about her face). This typically works for her with nearly ever man she encounters. She easily manipulates conversation and avoid answering problematic questions. When her charm and beauty fail her, her assertiveness tends to get the job done—and that's about the only thing that seems to work on Jack Whitlowe.

One of the greatest things about Page's portrayal as the Charmer is that, like many Playboys, her seduction methods don't get her very far with Jack. In fact, she's far less smooth with him than she's shown to be early on in the movie—as if his absolute goodness

323

disarms her of any charming and seductive assets, because he only cares about her heart. He often causes her to fumble over her words, and in what seems to be an act of desperation, she tends to revert to kissing him in order to get her way . . . though, if we're honest, Jack never seems to mind it.

Page resists falling for Jack, being as cruel and unfeeling at every turn—but it's clear that she's not doing a very good job of it. When Jack tells her he loves her, it acts as the breaking point for Page. She kisses him with her eyes closed (something that apparently indicates true affection) and nearly sleeps with him, before breaking things off because he's too good for her. She immediately returns home to tell her mother that she's dropping the con, after which she begins ignoring Jacks calls.

As she recognizes the goodness in Jack, Page begins to question the ethics of their cons. Multiple times she attempts to back out of the con, realizing that Jack doesn't deserve the pain—especially when she realizes that the only way to get any money out of him is by getting the deed to the bar which his dad left him. By their wedding night, it is clear that she has genuinely developed feelings for her, as she is heartbroken to set him up on their wedding night.

CHARMER KEY QUOTES

Max: You're not ready, Page.
Page: Yeah I'm so not ready that I already got him to say. I love you.
Max: I mean you're not ready to con a guy without falling in love yourself.
Page: Give me a break, I am in complete control.
Max: I saw the kiss. Your eyes were closed.
...
Page: I'm a pro, mother. And I'll prove it.

324

***

Jack: I scared you when I told you I loved you, didn't I?
Page: Jack, there is no love. It's just a trick of the brain—a combination of hormones and chemicals.

CINNAMON ROLL—reader's desire to find companionship, kindness, and support from their partner

Jack is pretty much portrayed as a kind-hearted man who gets caught up in the cons and deception of the Conners women. Though he is wealthy, he lives a humble and simple life. He is shown to be a thoughtful business owner, a good friend, and a seriously gracious romantic partner. Heck, even when Page is a total stranger—and a rude one at that—he's unrelenting in his goodness.

When Page first walks into his bar, she is demeaning and abrasive but Jack never throws it back at her. While still standing his ground, he doesn't cow down to her and he chooses to see the best in her.

While, Jack is undoubtedly, a total cinnamon roll, one of his most enjoyable traits is that, despite his goodness, he possesses a biting wit, that gives Page with her sarcasm a run for her money. Throughout their relationship, he takes her harsh words in stride, and somehow they still always end the conversation with kissing. As her deception draws out, it is clear that Jack is penetrating her walls with his kindness and genuine care for her.

On their wedding night, when Max tries to seduce him, he turns her down. From the beginning, he is resistant to spending time away from Jane, and he adamantly pushes her away before outright refusing. In a desperate ploy, max asks him to stay for one more drink. She ends up having to drug him, just to get him into the bed.

325

Even during the divorce proceedings, he puts up no fight, telling both lawyers and "Jane" (Page) that she will get whatever she wants.

Jack proves to be a fantastic foil to Page, and serves as the driving force for Page's own character arc in a way that feels neither unrealistic (at least not entirely) nor contrived.

CINNAMON ROLL KEY QUOTES

Bill (Jack's friend): You gotta give up on that girl, man. There's something…weird about her.
Jack: Yeah but that's what I liked.

***

Page: You're too good for me.
Jack: I think I'll be the judge of that.
Page: You have to trust me. I am not a good person.
Jack: No, you are good. You may not know it, but I do. You come on tough, but it's all just an act.

***

[While Max tries to seduce him]
Max (Betsy): Jane would never know, I promise.
Jack: Yeah, but I would. And I could never do that to someone I love.

THE ROMANCE WRITER'S ENCYCLOPEDIA SERIES

There's more to "Writing to Market" than calling your hero a Billionaire and putting him in a suit on the cover.

But what if you don't have time to read a dozen Small Town romances or a dozen Cowboy books or a dozen Nanny/Single Dad romances, hoping you can glean the patterns and expectations of these markets?

That's where we come in.

The Romance Writer's Encyclopedia is doing the legwork for you. Using our unique Framework Trope method, which separates tropes into categories based on how they impact your story, we examine each trope, explain why readers love it, and clue you in on the unspoken expectations of the trope, as well as some pitfalls you might encounter while writing.

This is far more than a book with an unexplained list of tropes or broad advice for writing romance. This is an encyclopedia, and each entry is detailed, but easy to understand. It will leave you excited and prepared to write a romance that delivers deep reader satisfaction based on the premise you've designed.

Whether you use the books to brainstorm, plot, edit, or help with marketing your books - this collection is sure to become one with a permanent place on your craft book shelf.

Learn more and see all the available titles in the series at www.thetropebooks.com

Volume 1: Romance Character Tropes

Volume 2: Romance Storyline Tropes

Volume 3: Romance Relational Tropes

Volume 4: Romance Setting Tropes

ABOUT THE AUTHORS

Best-selling author and marketing coach Tara Grace Ericson has published nearly twenty novels in Christian romance and romantic suspense. She was a Carol Award finalist for Best Christian Fiction by the American Christian Fiction Writers in 2022. Follow her at @taraericsonauthor on Facebook and Instagram. Her website is www.taragraceericson.com

Jessica Barber is the chief editor at New Life Editing Solutions where she offers editing and story coaching services for both traditionally and independently published authors. She is the author of *Beyond the Beats: How to Write a Romance Readers Can't Resist*. You can view her editing services at www.newlifeediting.com

Jessica and Tara co-founded The Inspired Author in 2022 with a vision of creating books, courses, and other resources to encourage and equip authors. Learn more at www.theinspiredauthor.net

MORE FROM
THE INSPIRED AUTHOR

**Beyond the Beats:
How to Write a Romance Readers Can't
Resist**

By Jessica Barber

Learn to grab readers' attention when you go beyond the story beats of the romance genre by harnessing the impact of the relationship arc, character arc, conflict, key moments, and other writing techniques.

Based on her experience working with dozens romance novelists over the last decade and insight from reading and studying thousands of romance novels, editor and story coach Jessica Barber has compiled the most lucrative advice for writing a well-developed, engaging novel that will have your readers begging for more.

This book will teach you:

> The guiding principles of the romance genre
> The basic structure and storytelling elements of romance
> Content expectations
> Ways to enhance and improve your storytelling

After reading this book, you can be confident that you will have the tools to take your novel from a good book to a book that readers can't put down.

**Prayers for Writers:
Guided Prayers for Every Aspect of
Your Writing Journey**

By Tara G. Ericson

This guided prayer journal is designed for Christian writers of all kinds. Any genre, any age, and any stage of publishing. Whether your writing is a hobby, a business, a forgotten passion, or something you've always wanted to try, this book is for you.

Inside you'll find prayers in four categories:

-Prayers for a Writer's Heart (Priorities, Faith, Humility, etc)
-Prayers for My Circle (Friends, Partner, Children, Teachers, etc)
-Prayers for a Writing Career (Success, Platform, Decisions, etc)
-Prayers for Specific Times (Evening Writing, Anxiety, Rejection, etc)

Along with tons of scripture, reflection questions and journaling space for you to invite the Lord into your writing.

With prayers about your craft, the people in your life, a writing career, and for specific times in your writing endeavors, you'll find countless ways to grow as a writer and as a follower of Jesus. Beautifully designed with journaling space and prayer prompts, this book was developed with the heart of a Christian writer in mind.

Made in the USA
Columbia, SC
07 December 2023

28017885R00192